The Pleasures of
# SLOW FOOD

# The Pleasures of
# SLOW FOOD

## Celebrating Authentic Traditions, Flavors, and Recipes

**CORBY KUMMER**

*Photographs by Susie Cushner*

**Preface by Carlo Petrini**
**Foreword by Eric Schlosser**

**CHRONICLE BOOKS**

SAN FRANCISCO

## PHOTOGRAPHER'S ACKNOWLEDGMENTS

The Slow Food movement shines a light on the passion and commitment of people throughout the world who continue bringing the traditions of the land and their cultures forward as they have for generations. Bless you all for the privilege and invaluable opportunity to learn and to see into the heart of the unique places you continue to cultivate. I wish to acknowledge these inspired, dedicated people who graciously opened their homes and their lives to us: Roberto Rubino and his farmers; Tom, Giana, and Fingal Ferguson; Elena and Raffaele Rovera; Laura and Franco Bera; the Garibaldis; Franca and her beautiful mother; the wonderfully warm Marino family; Jean-Pierre Grangé; the Descoubet family; Jean Lamothe and Marie Lamothe in France; Lothar and Heike in Lübeck; Paul Bertolli; Alice Waters, her assistant Christina, and the amazing chefs Alan, Russell, Gordon, Brian, and their staffs; to Judy Rodgers; June Taylor; Chad and Liz of Bay Village Bakery; Deborah Madison; Inniskillin's Karl Kaiser and Debra Platt; Michael O'Leary and Robert Hicks in Longboat Key; Ana Sortun in Cambridge, Massachusetts; Cindy and David Major in Vermont; the Dietrich family in Pennsylvania Dutch country; and Daniel Boulud from Daniel.

I would also like to express sincere gratitude for hard work, dedication, support, and perseverance from Judy, Teri, and Anna at my studio, and for perfect assistance from Roderick, Jon K., and David. For Jacqueline's generosity, and always to Jenna and Kayla for consistent encouragement, tolerance, and unconditional love during the past eight months.

This has been a magical project in every way, provided by my cherished Chronicle Books "family," which, for this project, was under the guidance and magnificent design of Pamela Geismar, and the editorial vision of Leslie Jonath. And to Corby Kummer for access to a wealth of treasures. Thank you.

—Susie Cushner

---

First Chronicle Books LLC paperback edition, published in 2008.
Text copyright © 2002 by Corby Kummer. Portions of the text in a different form first appeared in the *Atlantic Monthly* and *Gourmet*.
Photographs copyright © 2002 by Susie Cushner.

The Library of Congress has cataloged the previous edition as follows:
Kummer, Corby.
 The pleasures of slow food: celebrating authentic traditions, flavors, and recipes/Corby Kummer; preface by Carlo Petrini; foreword by Eric Schlosser; photographs by Susie Cushner.
  p. cm.
Includes index.
 ISBN 0-8118-3379-8
 1. Cookery. I. Title.
 TX652 .K86 2002
 641.5—dc21          2002002731

Manufactured in China
Designed by Pamela Geismar
Typesetting by Kristen Wurz

10 9 8 7 6 5 4 3 2 1

Chronicle Books LLC
680 Second Street
San Francisco, California 94107

www.chroniclebooks.com

ISBN 978-0-8118-6382-7

**FOR JA**
*Who made this,
and everything else,
possible*

## ACKNOWLEDGMENTS

This book is the result of two phone calls. The first came across a scratchy transatlantic wire from Patrick Martins, inviting me to the second Salone del Gusto, in Turin. A young man of relentless charm, Patrick managed to pull me away from the fascinating frenzy of food and artisans and push me into a low-ceilinged, overcrowded press room. An hour spent listening to Carlo Petrini, the founder of Slow Food, turned into five years of study, travel, and dedication to the ideals that I immediately realized I shared that day in Turin.

The second call was from the buoyant Leslie Jonath, at Chronicle Books, who thought that the article I wrote on the Salone for *The Atlantic* might make a book. She convinced me and her colleagues (a much harder task) that there was a book to be written, one inspired by but independent of the Slow Food movement. Against formidable obstacles, most notably a procrastinating author, Leslie pulled together her team to produce a book every member could be proud of—a tribute to her perseverance and unflagging enthusiasm.

Always inspiring, too, was my soul mate at Slow Food, Cinzia Scaffidi. Her role in this book, as at Slow Food headquarters, is incalculable. Mavi Negro cleared the way for the book to be written and was always its *dea ex machina*. Also at Slow Food, Laura Bonino, Roby Burdese, Barbara Carrara, Gigi Piumatti, and the Sardo men were unhesitatingly helpful. In New York, Patrick Martins, Serena Di Liberto, and Erika Lesser answered all questions with imagination and incredible speed, and with the help of Dick Bessey persuaded innocent interns to gather the information for the Source Guide.

Eric Schlosser wrote a stirring and eloquent foreword at a particularly busy moment, and gave astute editing suggestions in addition to encouragement and friendship.

Something like the movement itself, the book attracted a group of unlikely collaborators who were exactly right and brought out the best in one another. The first two were no accident. Pamela Geismar, art director of Chronicle, honored us all when she decided to design the book. She asked Susie Cushner to take the pictures—a momentous request. Susie quickly grasped the essence. I'm in awe of the belief, energy, and joy she brought to the book, and of the beautiful design Pamela crafted for it.

Friends told me that there was no better recipe tester in the Bay Area than Tasha Prysi, a former cook at Chez Panisse, but that she would doubtless be unavailable. Upon entering a kitchen to help prepare Chez Panisse's twenty-fifth anniversary party, I asked the first person I saw how to find the supervising chef. "Hi, I'm Tasha," she replied. She was indeed the best choice imaginable, with a great sense of how food should taste and how to put it within range of the home cook. Megan Anthony coordinated the far-flung chefs who so generously donated the book's recipes.

Sharon Silva offered text-editing guidance both conceptual and line by line. I and the book benefited from her clarity and skill. Carolyn Miller took charge of the precise task of recipe-editing. When I most needed fact-checking and typesetting assistance, two helpmeets miraculously appeared: Jennifer Villeneuve and Caitlin Riley. Each put her all into doing too much work in too little time, and doing it well. Lisa Campbell, at Chronicle, made sure all the pieces fit together.

I could not have dreamed of writing this book without the indulgence and support of the ideal family that is *The Atlantic Monthly*. They are wonderful friends and colleagues who make life and work a pleasure day by day. My editors at *Boston Magazine* kindly extended deadlines in the busy last months of book production. Rafe Sagalyn is the model of an agent—wise, encouraging, measured, active when it counts.

I'm deeply grateful to have family and friends who keep me afloat, who bear the interruptions in precious friendship that books mandate. In Italy, north to south: Nicola Turcato, Soly Benveniste, Faith Willinger, Ginevra Bruti-Liberati, the Tondo and Guerra-Watkins clans, Claudio and Benedetta Cavalieri, the bewitching Patience Gray. In the United States, west to east: Pam Hunter and Carl Doumani, Carol Field, Flo Braker, Peggy Pierrepont, the Hershes, Kate Jakobsen, Keith Alexander, the Kummers and the Lavitts, Fred Plotkin, Tony May, Maggie Simmons, Charles Mann, Erika Pilver, Nesli Basgoz, Margo Howard, Sheryl Julian, Ellen Kennelly, Kenneth Mayer, Rux Martin, the families Rosenbloom and Sedgwick, Dorothy Zinberg. Barbara Kafka ever prods me toward emotional and intellectual growth.

I won't name each of the artisans and chefs who unquestioningly welcomed Susie and me into their lives and souls with amazing, openhanded generosity. I can only hope that this book is an adequate tribute—one that might inspire others to follow their brave and loving example.

*—Corby Kummer*

# CONTENTS

Preface .........................................................................................9
Foreword .....................................................................................10

### THE MOVEMENT
What Is Slow Food? ....................................................................16
A Charismatic Founder Who Knew How to Have a Good Time ..............18
Creating Italy's Own Michelin Guide ...........................................20
The Decisive Moment: Militating against McDonald's....................20
Theory into Action: The Ark, the Presidium, and the Slow Food Award ........22
Outward Bound: Slow Food Abroad..............................................25
The Mecca of the Food World .....................................................26

### THE ARTISANS
**CHEESE:** Roberto Rubino, *Italy*.................................................31
**CHEESE:** Cindy and David Major, *Vermont* ...............................36
**MEAT:** Torsten Kramer, *Germany* ...........................................40
**MEAT:** Verna Dietrich, *Pennsylvania* .......................................43
**SALT:** João Navalho, *Portugal*................................................46
**SHELLFISH:** Michael O'Leary, *Florida*......................................51
**WINE:** Karl Kaiser, *Canada*...................................................55
**WINE:** André Dubosc, *France*.................................................61
**FRUIT:** Stephen Wood, *New Hampshire* ....................................65
**VEGETABLES:** Jim Gerritsen, *Maine* ........................................70
**BOTANICAL ARK:** Alan and Susan Carle, *Australia*.......................74

### THE RECIPES
Marino Family, Mulino Marino, *Cossano Belbo, Italy*.......................81
Garibaldi Family, Cà di Gòsita, *Liguria, Italy* ...............................84
Elena Rovera, Cascina del Cornale, *Cornale, Italy*..........................87
Lothar Tubbesing, Restaurant Lachswehr, *Lübeck, Germany*...............93
Georgette Dubos, Auberge de la Bidouze, *Saint-Mont, France*............97
Tom and Giana Ferguson, *Schull, County Cork, Ireland*....................101
Steve Johnson, The Blue Room, *Cambridge, Massachusetts*................106
Ana Sortun, Oleana Restaurant, *Cambridge, Massachusetts* ..............111
Daniel Boulud, Daniel, *New York, New York*...................................118
Ben and Karen Barker, Magnolia Grill, *Durham, North Carolina*..........122
Rick Bayless, Topolobampo and Frontera Grill, *Chicago, Illinois* ........127
Deborah Madison, *Santa Fe, New Mexico*.....................................134
Alice Waters, Chez Panisse, *Berkeley, California*............................138
Judy Rodgers, Zuni Café, *San Francisco, California* .......................147
Paul Bertolli, Oliveto Café and Restaurant, *Oakland, California*..........154
June Taylor, *Oakland, California* ................................................160
Elisabeth Prueitt, Tartine, *San Francisco, California*.......................165

Source Guide ............................................................................171
Index.......................................................................................173
Table of Equivalents....................................................................175

# PREFACE

EVERY TIME SLOW FOOD ARRIVES IN A NEW country, what happens is an exchange followed by rapid growth. New members "learn" our philosophy, yes, but the whole movement benefits from new ideas. Our own philosophy becomes more complex and more interesting.

I like the idea that this book arrives in the hands of so many people who don't yet know Slow Food. I'd like to think they'll find resonance in the marvelous stories of individual artisans and farmers, and also in the ideas of the movement—a sort of common denominator for their own needs as gourmets, as environmentalists, as people who care about the future of the planet. It's no longer possible to separate these concerns from the concerns of other people and other places. Everything and everyone are bound up together, today more than ever.

I'm grateful to the publishers of this book for being willing to bet time and money on these ideas of ours. And I sincerely admire—and always view with amused affection—the way the author has studied us over the years, with rigor and curiosity that don't let up. He is now one of the most effective ambassadors we have in the world. Americans who are already members are sure to recognize in this book everything they know about Slow Food. Readers who are not couldn't hope for a better guide than our old friend Corby. So here's to you, Corby, and the success of your comprehensive, beautifully written chronicle of our movement.

—*Carlo Petrini*
*President, Slow Food*

# FOREWORD

WHEN YOU ORDER A HAMBURGER, FRENCH fries, and a cola from a fast-food restaurant, here's what you're likely to get: A paper cup full of carbonated water, ice, sugar, corn syrup, food coloring, and "natural flavor." Frozen fries that were flavored with chemical additives, reheated in hydrogenated vegetable oil, salted, then placed beneath a heat lamp. A thin, frozen hamburger patty—containing meat from hundreds of different cattle, raised in as many as five different countries, ground together in gigantic vats at a distant processing plant—reheated on an automated grill. The ketchup and the pickle also contain flavor additives, manufactured at high-tech specialty chemical plants off the New Jersey Turnpike.

When you eat this meal, it tastes pretty good. It was carefully formulated to taste good. But twenty or thirty minutes later, there's an odd aftertaste, a subtle reminder that this food isn't like the food you make from scratch in your own kitchen. Fast food is an industrial commodity, assembled by machines out of parts shipped from various factories. In many ways it has more in common with a toaster oven or a fluorescent lamp than it does with a home-cooked meal. *Bon appétit.*

The Slow Food movement stands in direct opposition to everything that a fast-food meal represents: blandness, uniformity, conformity, the blind worship of science and technology. The McDonald's Corporation has a slogan, One Taste Worldwide, that perfectly encapsulates the stultifying, homogenizing effects of its global empire. Why would anyone want to live in such a world? What conceivable motive, other than the profit motive, would drive anyone to pursue one taste so ruthlessly? If fast food is the culinary equivalent of a sound bite, then Slow Food is an honest, thorough declaration of intent. Many tastes are better than one, this new movement says.

Critics of Slow Food claim that it is elitist and effete, too expensive for ordinary people, just the latest trend among foodies and gourmands. I would use a different set of adjectives to describe the movement: necessary and long overdue. Slow Foods are mainly peasant foods—dishes and ingredients that have been prepared the same way for centuries. They are time-tested. They spring directly from regional cultures and cuisines. They are not effete. Fast food stems from an entirely different sort of mass culture and mass production. It is a recent phenomenon. Although McDonald's has been around for more than half a century, it did not begin to rely on highly processed, frozen meals until the early 1970s. The centralization and industrialization of our food system has largely occurred over the past twenty years. And its huge social costs—the rise in food-borne illnesses, the advent of new pathogens such as *E. coli* 0157:H7, antibiotic resistance from the overuse of drugs in animal feed, extensive water pollution from feedlot wastes, and many others—have become apparent only recently. These costs are not reflected in the price of a burger and fries at the drive-through window. But they should be. Our fast, cheap food has proven to be much too expensive.

Corby Kummer is the ideal author to write about Slow Food. He can speak with great authority not just about food but also about politics, law, public-health issues, history, and literature. More important, he has good taste. Kummer understands the Slow Food movement's rationale, has long supported its aims, and is immune to hype.

Fast-food chains like McDonald's are a creation of the late twentieth century, and their charmless, plastic, bureaucratic worldview is rapidly becoming obsolete. People are beginning to realize that no industry is more important than the food industry. That all of human civilization is dependent on the ability to produce and consume the right foods. That what you eat defines you, intrinsically. The change from a disposable society to a sustainable one begins with the first bite. If you care about these things and all their implications, you will want to savor *The Pleasures of Slow Food.*

—*Eric Schlosser*

THE MOVEMENT

GIUSEPPE GARIBALDI HANDS WHITE-HOT CERAMIC saucers to his mother, Maria Ines D'Amico, who is hunched over the hearth of a woodburning fireplace so big it has its own little house. The hearth stands across from the shipshape stucco house of their family farm, at the top of a steep hillside in Liguria, on the Italian Riviera. Wearing a white gauze cap that keeps her long white hair away from the embers on the hot, hot stone floor and sets off the handsome features of her wide face, Maria Ines ladles just enough thin batter to coat the bottom of the saucer—a mold with an intricate raised pattern for *testaroli,* a kind of crepe famous in this part of paradise.

She stacks the saucers in piles of four on the hearth, expertly keeping them moving with iron tongs. Every so often she checks the two other dishes in the oven, both of them cooking in wide, shallow, time-battered aluminum pans covered by terra-cotta cloches that look like they might have been designed by Gaudí. To see into the pans, one of them holding a veal-and-potato stew and the other a huge round of bread that rises to fill the cloche, Maria Ines signals her son. He turns a crank connected to a chain that lifts each cover straight up, releasing the fragrances of rosemary and fresh-baked bread.

When Maria Ines judges the crepes done—when bubbles come to the surface and set, just like on pancakes—she expertly raps each one out onto a brick-red earthenware plate. Once there's a stack of eight or so, Giuseppe takes the plate into the kitchen across the way. There a woman a bit younger than his mother takes each *testarolo* and puts it pattern-side up on a serving dish, with the medieval design from the bottom of the saucer clearly embossed. She paints each crepe with a thick layer of the glory of Liguria—pesto sauce made from the delicate, tiny-leaved basil that grows only here, and from olive oil extracted from olives the mother and son tend and bring to the local press. *Parmigiano-Reggiano,* the world's greatest cheese, is made in the next region, and a goodly amount goes into the glistening gold-green sauce.

The woman in the kitchen stacks four *testaroli* at a time, the filling running down the sides in jeweled drips, and cuts wedges of the beautiful torte to go to the big wooden farm table in the next room. A dozen diners who minutes before were watching the hearth activity are now gathered round the table in eager expectation. They take the wedges in their hands and lick the pesto that oozes from the soft, thick crepes off their fingers.

As the diners bite into the pesto, pungent with garlic, unctuous from the oil and pine nuts, and the softened *testaroli* that hold the sauce like a sponge, mother and son are judging that the vast bread is cooked through, and the potatoes are browned enough to send to the table. The taste the guests will remember along with the pesto is the browned cubes of potatoes, crusty at the corners with a slight smokiness from the branches Giuseppe cut a few weeks earlier and let dry under the eaves of the shed for the hearth. The potato flesh is both pillowy and lightly resilient, with little bursts of steam that bathe the face with the fragrance of the rosemary and olive oil. It's a flavor that the guests, some of whom live just a few kilometers away, could find only at this table, on this hillside, served by this mother and son, with their monumental square faces out of a Renaissance fresco.

## WHAT IS SLOW FOOD?

Slow Food wants to save lives, and meals, like these. To do that, people like the Garibaldis must be able to keep farming the land and support themselves and their families. That wasn't so easy for Giuseppe, who worked as a stevedore in the nearby port of Genoa for seventeen years before he could afford to work full-time on the farm that had been in his widowed mother's family for generations. Even then, his savings weren't enough to keep the farm going. So he and his mother took a gamble on starting Cà di Gòsita, a small restaurant where locals long unable to eat hearth-baked *testaroli* can make their way up the winding narrow road to the big wooden farm table, with its spectacular views of Genoa and the Mediterranean beyond.

Slow Food hasn't adopted Giuseppe and Maria Ines, even though their farm is just a few hours from the movement's birthplace and headquarters in Bra, a small city in Piedmont, the northwest corner of Italy. The food they make and the way of life they are stubbornly trying to continue have existed for millennia, and Slow Food makes no claim to discovering them. It just wants to help them survive for millennia more. It is their very stubbornness Slow Food looks for—people who are betting on themselves and their ability to overcome the obstacles of the modern world, so that they can grow and share the food of a land to which they feel passionately connected.

Here's how Slow Food could help mother and son—the kind of concrete steps the international movement takes to keep local farms and restaurants and their unique flavors alive. If while still working on the docks Giuseppe had driven to Slow Food headquarters, he could have gathered a large amount of information about the rare crops and animal breeds that were farmed in his area, and how he could create a market for them. He could have learned which kinds of renovations local and European Union regulations required him to make—permanent walls for the hearth shed, for instance—and where to apply for loans both to make them and to fulfill his own desire for bigger windows that would give better views of the olive trees on the Ligurian hillsides all around.

Once mother and son had found a woman to help in the kitchen who had the taste of Liguria in her fingertips and the restaurant was up and running, local Slow Food chapters could hold meetings there and conduct tastings of, say, oil pressed from the olives of several local farms, or of heirloom vegetables. Or chapter members could gather at the hearth to learn from a local ceramicist how to cast the cloches that covered the veal-and-potato stew, and to watch Maria Ines practice a centuries-old cooking method.

Slow Food chapters, called convivia for their civilized and convivial bringing together of people who love food and traditions, are the lifeblood of the organization. The chapters show people who don't have a family farm to rescue—who don't have a scrap of land they can farm, let alone the time to farm it—how they can reconnect with the land every day by finding and cooking meat and vegetables raised by people like the Garibaldi family.

Slow Food is also a formidable worldwide nexus and distributor of information. Its authoritative guidebooks are the first place Italians look for advice on good wine and food wherever they're traveling, and its Web site is increasingly becoming the place that people who want a true taste of a particular city or region look to find the best suggestions.

And Slow Food could literally, not just virtually, bring artisans like Giuseppe and Maria Ines to the world at the grand conference-festivals it stages every two years in the Piedmontese city of Turin, the birthplace of Fiat and the financial and industrial capital of northern Italy. The Salone del Gusto (Hall of Taste), as the fantastic five-day carnival is called, has become the one international food fair that is a must for lovers of good food. It takes place in Fiat's first factory, a marvelous piece of industrial architecture that has a miniature racetrack where its first sports cars were tested. The aisles of the Salone are lined with hundreds of booths of artisanal-food producers and growers. Here a chef from Caracas meets a beekeeper from the mountains of Turkey, a vanilla grower from Chiapas meets a pastry chef from Athens.

At the Salone, dozens of seminars go on continuously during each of the five days—lessons and tastings of rare wines and artisanal cheeses, of ten kinds of chocolate from South America and Africa, of five kinds of pressed salmon roe, of six Trappist beers from Belgium. There are lunches and dinners cooked by chefs and artisans around the world using the ingredients they gathered at local farms and somehow got through customs. Every morning schoolchildren from around the country come for special guided tours and classes designed just for them, with many of the activities set up on the original racetrack. A corner-stone of Slow Food's mission is to show children what real food looks like when it comes out of the ground, and to make sure they steal greedy bites.

The commitment to education, apparent every minute of the intense, over-stimulating Salone, is obvious at the events held every day by convivia around the world. For several years Slow Food has been planning to mount its own degree-conferring institute—a complex including a hotel and restaurant in a beautiful neo-Romanesque former royal hunting lodge a few miles from its headquarters. The degree will be called a Master of Taste, and it will be awarded to students of all ages from around the world who learn to recognize what makes a local food local: how to taste the air and earth in every bite of cheese and every sip of wine, and how to help keep those tastes alive in the modern world.

Slow Food has reached people in a way no other environmental or gastronomic group or movement has because it does not seek to freeze traditions or turn places like Giuseppe and Maria Ines's tiny hilltop farm restaurant into living museums. It wants such places to serve as examples—to send someone back to Malmö or Adelaide in search of the most delicious thing that comes out of the ground or farm kitchen. The movement combines urgent issues like protecting the environment and cataloging and preserving indigenous crops with ways to enjoy foods and traditions that are disappearing with the speed at which McDonald's opens new restaurants. It is fiercely dedicated to maintaining biodiversity.

Unlike other environmental groups, however, Slow Food tells members to prepare for "suitable doses of guaranteed sensual pleasure and slow, long-lasting enjoyment." If you have a good time while you eat, the movement argues, you'll have better meals. And a better life.

### A CHARISMATIC FOUNDER WHO KNEW HOW TO HAVE A GOOD TIME

To understand why Slow Food's message has gotten through to so many people—while other food and wine societies, however well meaning, have seemed like irrelevant ways to show off—you need to meet Carlo Petrini, the founder of the movement, and learn something about the radicalized Italy that shaped him. The Slow Food story is one of politics, ideals, singing, and unabashed rustic pleasure.

Slow Food had jolly beginnings. It started in 1980, with a small band of left-wing activists telling their comrades that pleasure was permissible. As Petrini saw it, the people's movement was intimately linked with the people's culture. Born in 1949 in Bra, Petrini watched his family and the neighbors in the countryside of the Langhe, as his corner of Piedmont is recognized, lovingly and obstinately raise and produce the foods for which the region was known: polenta, chestnuts, honey, hazelnuts, apples, cheese, earthy and pungent white truffles, magnificently intense Barolo wine. He heard their work songs in the lyrical, French-accented Piedmontese dialect, and lustily sang along to the accordions someone would always bring to an end-of-harvest party. He shared their rough, mountain-hewn humor and was greatly influenced by the subversive humor of the satirist Dario Fo, a close friend who went on to win a Nobel Prize in literature.

Even in his early twenties, Petrini had an unusual talent for speaking with extreme clarity and for listening carefully, his huge brown eyes seeming to comprehend, priestlike, the true intent that lay behind the words of anyone speaking to him. The young sociology student threw himself into the political militancy of the early 1970s. In 1975, at the age of twenty-six, he founded Radio Bra Red Waves, the first left-wing, independent radio station in his region of Italy (and only the second radio station to break the state monopoly).

Music and humor were as much in Petrini's blood as politics. A Piedmontese folk-music festival he established sent musicians into schools and even people's houses to bring them the songs of the region; with several friends he started a theater troupe that performed satirical sketches and political comedy. Their performances brought out a hard truth. The left wing didn't want to enjoy itself too much—at least not when Vietnam and Cambodia were being ravaged and nuclear weapons were proliferating. "I came to understand," Petrini says, "that those who suffer for others do more damage to humanity than those who enjoy themselves. Pleasure is a way of being at one with yourself and others."

Petrini practices what he preaches: he's a big, shaggy, bearded man who clearly loves to eat as much as to declaim.

How to sell sensual pleasure to activists who find it bourgeois and decadent? In 1980, Petrini and his friends decided to start a new branch of an established national network that helped chiefly blue-collar workers. The idea was different from every other branch's, and in its own way was as revolutionary as anything their fellow Italian activists were calling for in remote parts of the world.

Petrini wanted to reawaken knowledge and esteem of country foods and wines that were at risk of disappearing as the people of the Langhe abandoned their hillside farms to go work in factories. Piedmont, birthplace of the Italian car, had always been the industrial engine of Italy. His group wanted to apply the region's hardheaded practicality to saving its own gastronomic and agricultural patrimony.

The friends opened a modest restaurant in the center of Bra, the Osteria del Boccondivino, to serve good, honest food at low prices. They held boisterous suppers that lasted until dawn, joining together pleasure and learning. All this was in a spirit opposite to the one national gourmet society then extant, a gentleman's club that listed to the right. From the start the group would combat every elitist tendency, every overpriced wine and fancified food. Any ritual smacking of secret societies would be ridiculed. Women were welcome, and so were people without much money to spend. Simple, good food of the land and bonhomie were values in themselves, the friends said. They distrusted "moralistic revolutionaries" and, worse, "anyone who doesn't laugh."

## CREATING ITALY'S OWN MICHELIN GUIDE

A good-time joviality was part of the founding spirit, but so was education. Petrini had started writing about food and wine soon after college. His samizdat radio broadcasts were both engaging and instructive, and much of the reason that people were drawn to him. The group organized seminars dedicated to the culture of Barolo and the truffle, with the guidance of not just connoisseurs but also philosophers, historians, and sociologists. Music and laughter were primary components. But the goal was also to draw strong connections between pleasure and where food came from and the rural life behind it.

Linking politics, history, sociology, anthropology, and philosophy with the fruits of the countryside was still a new concept in the Italy of the early 1980s. One trailblazing magazine did combine all these disciplines—the Milan-based *La Gola*. Petrini and friends admired it so much that in July 1986 they named themselves Arcigola. At a first convention in the storybook castle of Barolo, seventy-two founding members elected Petrini president. The dinner, one of many, lasted until dawn.

Arcigola went to work attracting national members, reaching far beyond wine seminars. In 1987, it published the first issue of a new kind of wine guide, as an insert in the left-wing newspaper *Il Manifesto*. The guide was called *Gambero Rosso* (Red Shrimp), to assert its ideological origins. The first Slow Food newsletter was published in collaboration with the left-wing newspaper *L'Unità*. *Gambero Rosso* experienced a huge, immediate success, and from 1988, its first year, its comprehensive annual evaluation of Italian wines became the internationally authoritative guide. Its highest rating—three glasses, like Michelin's three stars—became synonymous with best quality. Wine makers continue to fear the guide, awaiting the annual ratings with equal parts hope and apprehension.

The next step was to extend *Gambero Rosso*'s success to restaurants, a move that helped lay the foundation for Slow Food. Instead of "innovative" restaurants that turned their backs on traditional foods and looked to France and Asia, Arcigola combed the country for *osterie*—home-style trattorias, roadside restaurants, and farmhouse inns open whenever the farm schedule allowed. These meeting places serving simple, seasonal, inexpensive food long held together village life and helped define local identity. But like so much artisanal food, they were at risk as people left villages to work in cities.

The first in a series of Arcigola travel and restaurant guides appeared in 1989. These unpretentious guides, which presented the unvarnished truth and the right places to eat, brought the group national visibility and attracted members from all over Italy. They also provided a financial base that helped make possible all the other initiatives.

## THE DECISIVE MOMENT: MILITATING AGAINST MCDONALD'S

The decisive moment—the sudden bursting from the chrysalis—took place in 1989, when Arcigola and most of right-thinking, left-leaning Italy looked with horror at plans to build a McDonald's in the heart of Rome. Sometimes it's easier to see what you're losing when a usurper stares you right in the face. McDonald's entered Italy very late, at the end

of 1985. Rather than start in the hinterlands, it focused on large cities. Many Italians were disturbed by the invasion and wanted to wage immediate war. Arcigola members took part in demonstrations at the Piazza di Spagna, at the foot of the Spanish Steps, where McDonald's planned to open.

The leadership knew that protests like these would not advance the movement's own battle very far. Instead of employing guerrilla warfare, it devised a long-term strategy to counter fast food with an alternative. The goals, pursued with new focus and new urgency, would be the ones to which it had already dedicated itself: saving dishes and foods from the flood of homogenization, rescuing modest restaurants serving genuine food.

This was war, yes, but a war that would require patience, ingenuity, and large quantities of good food. It would also require a new name, to show the scope of its ambition and the urgency of its mission: Slow Food.

"Globalization" did not yet exist as a term describing a worldwide threat, but Slow Food knew what it needed to oppose. McDonald's symbolized a disturbing global split that Arcigola's founders had lamented from the start. On one side of the gulf were rich consumers who looked for good, genuine products cultivated by poor people—who only got poorer by continuing their traditional practices. On the other were poor people constrained to buy bad food at cheap prices made possible by immensely potent industrial producers. Slow Food wanted to bridge the gap. Eating a new food on every street of the world was the best response to the McDonald's challenge.

The galvanizing arrival of a clear enemy focused a fledgling movement that had already won the allegiance of thousands of Italians. Now it could rally members from neighboring countries—from all over the world. The new name and the new challenge made an international thrust imperative. A call to arms was issued, and a meeting place set: the Opéra Comique in Paris, a place where subversive wit had flourished for centuries. In December 1989, delegates from fifteen countries ratified the newly named Slow Food manifesto and approved the movement's symbol: the snail, a "small, cosmopolitan, and prudent" creature and an "amulet against speed." The Slow Food movement quickly assumed the form that won it worldwide support, the form in which it exists today.

## THEORY INTO ACTION: THE ARK, THE PRESIDIUM, AND THE SLOW FOOD AWARD

Three initiatives are embedded in the Slow Food DNA—three ways to help people grow, produce, and consume the right kind of food. The ideas are intuitive and easy to grasp. And once you grasp them, you want to join in.

The initiatives are the Ark, a directory of endangered foods around the world that members rescue by enjoying them; the Presidia, grassroots organizations that Slow Food helps with advice and money as a way of making Ark foods available to the general public; and, finally, the Slow Food Award, the Nobel Prize of biodiversity, which brings inspiring artisans and agricultural activists, mostly from the Third World, to international attention and gives them concrete assistance.

Everything must first happen locally. A leader volunteers to establish a convivium and bring in members. Then, with the help of the members, the leader finds regional culture as manifest in, say, the perfume of a wine or of a bread fresh out of a bakery oven. The convivium invites the wine maker or baker to explain to the members how the product is made and to share her or his personal history. The job of the chapters is to encourage the maintenance of local food and wine traditions; to safeguard the local agricultural patrimony against environmental degradation; to help consumers find good food and wine at a reasonable price; and to research and promote gastronomic pleasure with a "smiling, tolerant style." Leaders and members alike donate their time.

The endangered food and wine identified by a convivium can, through a nomination and judging process, climb aboard the Ark of Taste. Slow Food announced the creation of the Ark in 1996, and since then it has grown to include hundreds of cheeses, meats, fish, fruits, and vegetables, and the foods that can be cooked and cured using them.

To qualify for inclusion in the Ark, a food must first be of exceptional quality and flavor. This may sound obvious, but just because a food is local and homemade doesn't mean it's particularly good or noteworthy. Slow Food members and friends in many countries submit nominations. Then committees of experts and other Slow Food friends, including journalists, historians, scientists, cooks, and farmers, take a closer look, and welcome the food aboard the Ark once it passes inspection.

An Ark food must be made from local raw materials, preferably from plants and animals native to the region. The method of preparation must be traditional and by hand, or as close to handmade as possible. Either the raw materials or the food itself must be closely linked to the place it is made, in a bond that can be environmental, socioeconomic, or historical. The scale of production should be small, the quantity of production limited. The food must be in real or potential danger of extinction.

Identifying, researching, and cataloging this treasury is a daunting enough task. But Slow Food is ever vigilant to avoid becoming a zoo, where exhibits are lovingly maintained and the essential life has been drained away. Slow Food wants to celebrate the soul *and* keep the body alive.

Ark foods must live in the modern world—must withstand the threats posed by bland, synthetic, mass-produced, and menacingly cheap food. To defend the Ark, Slow Food took the further step of creating the Presidium, a word roughly equivalent to "fort" or "garrison." Presidia are mini–SWAT teams that put at the disposal of the artisans the mighty publicity resources of Slow Food and look for inventive ways to help them.

The first line of defense is publicity, at which Slow Food excels. It compiles and distributes on the Slow Food Web site a list of the remaining producers of each food aboard the Ark and posts their names along with a description of what makes them special. Then it looks for places that can serve and sell Ark foods, starting with local inns and cafés that are able to use them every day. Slow Food awards these modest but elemental eating places "special recognition" by recommending them in its best-selling guides and on its Web site—a place to which members and food lovers the world over increasingly turn for advice on where to eat.

Slow Food asks something more of larger restaurants: to adopt an Ark food and feature it in special dishes. The pleas for adoption go farther afield. A Presidium asks towns and regions to adopt a local Ark food and promote its awareness and use. The scale, as with cafés and restaurants, then gets larger and more ambitious: from the local town hall to the statehouse to the very seat of the nation's government. Presidia look for bureaus and organizations that can help support farmers and producers of artisan foods, and, especially

in Europe, for intergovernmental groups that are concerned with agriculture and nutrition and thus equipped to give a helping hand.

A Presidium helps by supplying assistance to cut through bureaucratic tangles caused by, for example, hygiene rules created for big businesses rather than small artisans. A typical example is the summertime alpine cheese maker who wants to sell legally the cheese he makes in a traditional cabin, without installing regulation bathrooms for men and women. Although this is possible under European Union laws, the paperwork required for the necessary variance is cumbersome and confusing. Slow Food undertakes this chore.

The assistance can be in the form of able-bodied helpers. A Presidium offers technical and financial help in finding and training apprentices to learn and practice what could soon be a lost art. In some cases a Presidium finds teachers, rather than apprentices, who can instruct an artisan how to make a product the old-fashioned way—mortadella sausage, for example, the fat grandfather of all bologna, without any chemical additives. A Slow Food committee searched out people who knew the secrets of the lost art and found butchers willing to revive it. Then Slow Food publicized the reappearance of additive-free mortadella at chapter events and inspired press accounts all over the world.

Slow Food's newest, and in some ways its most ambitious, initiative is the Slow Food Award, established in 2000. Concern for the environment and the dwindling reserves of the genetic diversity that keep plants and animals healthy are a Slow Food building block. The award is Slow Food's way of focusing attention on the people who preserve biodiversity as it relates to food—people who may in the process save whole villages and ecosystems.

This diversity resides principally in the Third World, and a turn toward the developing world marks another important change in Slow Food's course. In 2001, the second group of fifteen nominees for five "special prizes" (everyone is called a winner) was chosen mostly from Central and South America, Africa, and India. With the second "edition" of the award, Slow Food also decided to create a Presidium for each nominee. This intervention to help conserve the prizewinners' plants, animals, and foods will by necessity be local and direct. Slow Food created a new foundation to enable the Presidia to work on the essential local level, far from Italian headquarters. Local members will help raise money by, for instance, asking restaurants using an Ark food to donate a percentage of all sales to the foundation.

Slow Food headquarters gives convivia outside Italy financial support. Its resources come mainly from membership dues, sales of its guidebooks, and corporate grants. In its home country, industrial and regional support has made possible Slow Food's most audacious plans. So far this support has come without strings, unless you consider prominent logos and banners strings. Chapters in other countries are less fortunate, and must scramble to find enlightened corporate and government sponsors. In places where people don't grow up knowing that food and the land it grows on are an integral and sacred part of life—that is, outside Italy and France and a few other European countries—corporations want to see immediate results for their financial help. Finding sponsorship that allows the realization of ambitious plans without being compromised is always a balancing act, one that Petrini manages with delicacy and unique skill. In response to anyone who wonders at his ability to line up corporate sponsorship for rural and defiantly uncommercial traditions, he says, "I haven't sold my soul yet, and at my age it's too late anyway." The future of Slow Food will rely on leaders with this kind of skill and personal integrity.

**OUTWARD BOUND: SLOW FOOD ABROAD**

Even at the signing of the first manifesto in Paris, Slow Food had a strong and vocal international following. People all over Europe soon established chapters, staging festive and educational meetings and dinners. When a critical mass of chapters establish themselves, a country acquires a national office of its own, with a modicum of autonomy and a charge to produce its own educational newsletters and events. Until recently only Germany, long the country second in membership to Italy, and Switzerland had their own national offices. The newest national office is in France, which awoke late to a movement originating in another country (*Sacré bleu!*). But it did awake, and French chapters are growing.

The largest and most ambitious international growth has been in the United States. Since opening its own national office in 2000 under the strong leadership of Patrick Martins, a New Yorker who spent several years at Bra headquarters helping run international activities, Slow Food USA has energetically added chapters. It quickly passed Germany as the world's second country in membership: seventy chapters within two years, compared with forty in Germany over a decade. The trailblazing regions were northern California and the Northeast, but the South (New Orleans and the Research Triangle of North Carolina in particular), the Midwest, and much of the West followed fast.

The U.S. push is for purity, informed by the vision embodied by Alice Waters, the founder of Chez Panisse and from the start a leading and passionate voice of Slow Food USA. Environmental awareness, sustainable agriculture, and especially education of young children—most of whom will otherwise know only mass-produced and especially fast food—have been its urgent calls. And Slow Food USA soon set about naming fruits, vegetables, and animal species to the Ark, mounting as its first Presidium that most emblematic American food—the turkey, which, like most foods in America, was appropriated and denatured by industry but still exists in noble, wild, and tasty forms.

## THE MECCA OF THE FOOD WORLD

All of Slow Food's initiatives have been announced at the Salone del Gusto, Slow Food's most visible worldwide activity and the inspiration for much of its worldwide growth. The simple urgency and appeal embodied in the Ark, announced at the 1996 Salone, was one of several breakthroughs that helped push Slow Food into international consciousness and attract thousands of new members.

The original idea for the Salone was a kind of mega-meeting, with several days of activities morning to night of the kind a typical chapter might organize every month or so: visits to local producers, "taste laboratory" sessions focused on appreciating just one product, dinners with instruction on wine, cheese, and cured meats. That such a huge convention could come together is testament to Petrini's charm and political finesse: it helped greatly that he was friendly with top executives at Fiat, who eased the way into using its converted first factory as convention quarters, and that he found a soul mate in Enzo Ghigo, the president of the powerful and rich Piedmont region. But the reason the world sets aside time to come to each Salone is that it's so much fun.

Today Slow Food counts seventy thousand members in more than forty-five countries. Maintaining all these initiatives and these dozens of chapters calls for a large staff—including a hundred people at the headquarters in Bra, a marvelous eighteenth-century palazzo where the original Osteria del Boccondivino still serves local food, at modest prices, in the wisteria-laden courtyard. The young people who fly in and out of the offices and buzz around Carlo Petrini lead a life that is anything but slow. But then, Petrini, at work in a serene, frescoed office in the palazzo, has long said that in the modern world "to be slow just to be slow is stupid." The secret is to take the time to learn, to enjoy, and to savor.

THE ARTISANS

THE ARK AND ITS FORTIFYING PRESIDIA COME alive only with stories of the artisans who have bravely decided to swim against the prevailing tides and practice crafts their mothers and fathers abandoned in the face of economic realities—or never learned, in the midcentury global rush to join the postwar boom. The charming, eccentric, varied stories of these women and men, many of them young and educated by their hardworking parents for a profession "better" than growing and producing food, are Slow Food's most precious repository. They are also its secret weapon in winning new adherents.

Here are ten of those stories, grouped two by two, as befits an Ark. They are paired not by sex but by broad category: cheeses, meats, salt and shellfish, wines, and fruits and vegetables. Most categories pair a European with a non-European producer, to show the important differences between a world in danger of losing its heritage and a world in danger of never developing one to lose. The last category, fruit and vegetables, describes two New England farmers reawakening traditions that had been a backbone of America's agricultural economy, betting that the lure of forgotten and superior flavors will keep their lovingly tended land safe from developers. Both Old and New Worlds risk losing the true flavors they still possess, as ruthlessly efficient production smoothes the deliciously rough edges of local food.

The people described here exemplify the founding ideals of Slow Food and its defining initiatives: the Ark, a directory of the world's endangered foods, and the Presidia, the garrisons that help build and sustain the markets that will keep those foods competitive in the modern world. Not all of these farmers and artisans are formal members of the Slow Food movement; the very fact that some of them do not formally take part in Slow Food activities shows the reach and power of the group's philosophy. Whether or not their foods and wines have been named to the Ark or are protected by a Presidium, these enterprising and committed artisans encourage fellow farmers and cooks to join them in demonstrating why handmade, local foods taste so much better.

The last couple is pointing the way of the future for both Slow Food and farmers on every continent—and especially in the Third World, the new focus of Slow Food activities. For their efforts at rescuing the rain forest's endangered plants, this couple, on the other side of the world from Slow Food headquarters, won the Slow Food Award. Without the passion and unflagging work of all the award winners, there will be no more Ark to fortify.

Nothing tastes as divine as milk-white ricotta trembling in its basket mold, wet and a little warm. It's custard from heaven.

A morning at the Di Gilio farm, in the sere, majestic, rocky mountaintops of Basilicata, south of Rome, begins with a dawn delivery of fresh cow's and sheep's milk. One of the four weather-beaten brothers who run the farm pours the milk in fat white streams from metal jugs into a steel tub. The milk is heated and coagulated in a stainless-steel kettle and left to mature in wooden vats until the late afternoon.

Another brother makes ricotta from the whey of cow's and sheep's milk, patiently stirring the coagulated milk and then ladling the tender curds into white perforated plastic tubs. He keeps the fresh cheese moist by placing the cooled tubs on steel racks covered with a quarter-inch depth of fresh water. As fast as he can arrange them, his sister-in-law transfers the dripping tubs onto wide plastic racks and loads them into the back of her tiny station wagon. Without so much as a good-bye, she slams shut the doors and sets off on a winding, steep route to deliver still-warm ricotta to farmhouses where the children have just left for school.

Other farms up and down Italy make ricotta nearly this wonderful. But no one else makes the straw-gold basketball-sized *caciocavallo podolico*, which looks like something alive, responsive, and giving when it is sliced open. The deep, buttery color alone invites you to taste it. In the mouth it is fragrant, pliant, herbal.

Slow Food placed *caciocavallo podolico*, named for the very rare and very local Podolico cow, on its first list of nominations for foods that belong in its Ark of Taste, declaring it one of Italy's greatest and most endangered cheeses. The Di Gilio brothers raise Podolico cows, and also sheep and goats, a half-hour drive from the pathbreaking Experimental Institute for Agricultural Research, a special part of the region's state-funded university. This institute isn't limited to fresh-faced college-age students. It has instead sought out farmers and cheese makers like the Di Gilio brothers and shown them how to modernize their cheese-making rooms, improve their cheese-making methods, and preserve their wonderfully moldy, wood-beamed ripening cellars.

**CHEESE**
*Roberto Rubino*
**ITALY**

Watching the brothers make *caciocavallo*, which they do with the milk they coagulated in the morning, is like watching a practiced acrobatics act. The cheese is worked using the *pasta filata* method, as are mozzarella and provolone. *Filata,* or "threaded," refers to the heating of cheese curds to form a rubbery ball that is kneaded, stretched, and knotted in very hot water. This is where the brothers show their fearless technique, born of years of experience and a little help from the institute. The stretching and knotting takes not just experience but also considerable strength: the strings of curd are as resistant as strong elastic bands.

*Caciocavallo* has an extra step that its cousins do not, a step that can lead to greatness: the curd is left to ripen in wooden vats for several hours before being kneaded and pulled. The timeworn wooden vats are the kind of furniture people hope to snap up for a song from unsuspecting old farmers and use as planters and mail trays. They are irreplaceable. That wood holds bacteria, which are essential to the flavor of the cheese. Not surprisingly, wood is frowned on by the European Union, so cheese makers must

obtain a special permit to use wood in any phase of cheese production. Keeping this kind of tradition alive in the face of bureaucratic challenges is where Slow Food and that institute down the road are indispensable.

The institute is headed by Roberto Rubino, a tall, handsome man with a round face and a full black mustache. Rubino looks like the hero of an early 1960s Italian neorealist film, except that he smiles a lot. He even gestures like an Italian movie star, with big, sweeping arm movements and that language of the hands only Italians know.

Rubino has been something of a hero in a slow-moving, isolated southern region that has changed little since those films were made. With minimal money but a good deal of entrepreneurial spirit and energy, he has created a fiefdom to protect and promote excellent, endangered cheeses that distill the dry, fresh mountain air. The school and mini-empire he has created won him one of the first Slow Food Awards. So impressed was the leadership with his work that they have made him a trusted adviser—a great honor, given that a founder of Slow Food and one of its most tireless representatives and educators, Piero Sardo, is among the world's leading authorities on Italian cheeses.

*Caciocavallo podolico* is Rubino's calling card—the cheese he can slice for any skeptic who doubts any of his theories about how best to prepare southern Italy for the future, about native breeds being the only ones suited to the local climate and terrain, and, most of all, about the crucial difference that milk from cattle allowed to graze makes to the flavor and quality of cheese.

Much of southern Italy is unknown not only to the rest of the world but also to most of Italy. Basilicata is rural and hard to reach, locked in the mountains. Startlingly shaped rock formations called *calanques*, the result of thousands of years of earthquakes and volcanoes, jut out

of hillsides. The land is so windy that even trees don't grow on it.

It is also locked in time—specifically the early 1960s, when the Italian government noticed that the region was poor and underdeveloped and missing out on the postwar boom that was transforming the economies of the north. The government gave money to help the region build industry, but that didn't happen. The problem, as Rubino saw it when he was earning a degree in agrarian sciences at the University of Naples, was that people who had never done anything besides farm didn't know how to handle a sudden influx of funds.

Rubino didn't know much about cheese, but he did care deeply about farmers and centuries-old traditions that he saw being torn apart by attempts to turn the land and its people into something they were not. He tried to think of a way to keep people on the land without trying to turn them into northern-style industrialists. "The secret is in reading the landscape," he says.

Mountainsides like these, with plenty of fragrant wild herbs and fresh summer climates, are ideal for transhumance, the memorably named practice of moving herds of sheep, cows, or goats from lowland stalls in the winter to high outdoor pastures in the summer. The incentive for a shepherd to travel by foot for many days or even weeks, alone with his animals and sleeping where he might, was free summer forage. Under Spanish domination, which lasted in this part of Italy for most of the 1600s and 1700s, shepherds had permission to carry arms when other citizens did not: animals might attack their flocks, robbers might attack them.

In Basilicata today, flocks still move from plains to mountains in the summer. But the sheep are herded by truck drivers on highways, rather than by shepherds on country roads. Landowners here are still largely absentee city dwellers, as they have been since the days of ancient Rome: even with the very recent arrival of highways, Rome is still a six-hour drive away.

Rubino was born with a can-do energy associated with the north and a wiliness associated with the south. He understood mountain culture and the south, having grown up outside Battipaglia, a town in the plains below Naples that is today the world capital of buffalo milk mozzarella. The region around Naples—Campania,

hillsides, in a village aptly named Bella. He searched out examples of endangered native livestock and gave them protected homes in pristine barns so that they could produce breeding stock to supply local farmers and eventually replace the unsuitable imported animals his predecessors had cosseted. He looked for ways

next door to Basilicata—was historically poor, too. But the fact that Battipaglia was able to make *mozzarella di bufala* world famous, and to maintain the quality of a traditional product using animals uniquely suited to the land (water buffalo) gave Rubino ideas for what to do when he arrived to work at the Experimental Institute for Agricultural Research in Potenza, the capital of Basilicata.

The institute, an offshoot of the agricultural department of the region's university, had been moved to the city in the late 1950s as part of the whole region's attempt to be modern. Upon becoming director, in 1982, Rubino began demodernizing it by moving it back to its original home—a beautiful model farm in rolling

to make local breeds pay. This is the only means by which rare animals can truly lose their endangered status.

The way he hit upon was cheese. The region's isolation had been a blessing, in preserving great cheeses made with the milk of animals able to thrive in difficult conditions. But those animals naturally produced less milk than breeds that had been imported for seventy years, and the animals themselves were disappearing. If Rubino could create a mystique around the too-well-kept secrets of the region's great cheeses—and make people crave *caciocavallo podolico* the way they do the buffalo milk mozzarella of his hometown—he could preserve the animals and the landscape of his adopted territory.

Quality depends on milk, and only quality could attract a worldwide market. Rubino first had to convince farmers to raise superior local cows in place of more profitable breeds. He invited farmers to his beautiful model barns, to learn how best to use milking equipment. Then he sought out artisans who still had the expertise and ripening traditions that were disappearing by the season. He wanted to teach cheese makers how to make good cheese again.

It took twenty years to raise the money to build a school and find the help, but today the cheese-making laboratory at the Bella institute is full of gleaming equipment. The teachers are artisans who have trained with cheese makers throughout the region and elsewhere in Italy— "abroad," to southerners. The students are farmers and craftsmen who might never have had much formal education, and for whom it is difficult to leave the farm for even a few days. Being taught by peers who take them and their work seriously gives them new respect for what they do.

The next step was showing cheese makers how to ripen cheese in cellars and caves, an art that was dying in Basilicata. Rubino found a mountainside cave that had once been used for aging, and started putting into it cheese made in the teaching lab, transforming the cave into a kind of auxiliary classroom. Word spread among farmers that the institute was a place where you could learn something. Farmers now come to Bella from around the country for short courses.

To put his ripening curriculum to the test, Rubino went to the place that first put Basilicata on the world map—a lovely and serene hill town called Moliterno, full of natural cheese-ripening caves where pecorino can develop a full, piquant flavor. So famous was its cheese that in the New York of a century ago Moliterno was synonymous with sheep's milk cheese. For nearly a hundred years, the hill town was left to its breezy solitude, until an ambitious young woman named Angela La Torraca was elected mayor and caught wind of Rubino's dreams of putting Moliterno cheese back on the world stage.

Rubino and the mayor discovered that a handsome palace, already the property of the town, contained a buried treasure: a cellar that had been Moliterno's most important pecorino ripening cave during its glory days. The mayor came up with the money needed to clear out the old town records and decades' worth of bric-a-brac. Rubino found cheese makers willing to consign cheeses to the care of craftsmen trained at his institute, who would age the pecorino for the months and years needed to reach greatness. That cheese is still under tender care, with the hopes that it will once again be famous in New York.

A role on the world stage is what Rubino seeks for these cheeses. In 1994, he set up yet another group, the one that will likely have the longest-lasting results—a nonprofit organization called Cheeses Under the Sky (ANFOSC is the acronym in Italian), to defend cheese made from grazing animals. Rubino's goal is to put an internationally recognized symbol on the label of every cheese made from the milk, preferably unpasteurized, of pasture-fed animals. ANFOSC has already achieved something of world significance. It publishes a magazine, *Caseus,* that is probably today's most informative guide for cheese artisans. Both Slow Food and the American Cheese Society have begun distributing *Caseus* to their members.

The great cheeses Rubino discovered in his adopted region, like *caciocavallo podolico,* have only increased his conviction that grass is good. "Everyone dismissed this landscape as degraded, of no use to people or animals," he says, driving from the Bella institute to watch the Di Gilio brothers stir a vat of cheese with a tall, thick wooden rod. "Look how gorgeous it is, how clean. Can you imagine bad milk coming from this?"

The milking parlor at Major Farm, a weathered wood cabin on a long and verdant rise, looks like an illustration for a lullaby about counting sheep. Fourteen sheep at a time scamper from an adjoining barn onto a knee-high platform and calmly put their heads into metal headlocks so that they can be milked. Then David Major pulls a lever like the

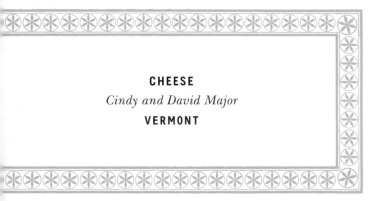

**CHEESE**
*Cindy and David Major*
**VERMONT**

one on a voting booth to release the sheep, who scamper out as the next fourteen come in.

Great cheese has always been made with great milk, and Major and his wife, Cindy, want both. They know what Roberto Rubino knows—that milk is better if the cow or sheep or goat grazed on green grass under an open sky. The cheese the Majors will make with the milk from those scampering sheep, who grazed in the storybook (and now very valuable) hills near Putney, Vermont, is a big proud wheel called simply Vermont Shepherd. It's America's finest sheep's milk cheese, with a firm but creamy texture, beautiful pale straw color, and the sweet, nutty overtones that come only from wild grass.

For that full spectrum of flavors to shine through, the milk not only must be from grazing animals but also must be raw—milk whose flavor-giving bacteria haven't been killed by pasteurization. This is another thing Rubino and the Majors know.

The matter is urgent in America, where the huge dairy industry is leading a worldwide fight to ban raw milk in cheese. Before World War II, almost all American cheese was made with raw milk, as it was in Europe for hundreds of years,

with no ill effects to people's health. Lactic acid in milk and the salt used to flavor and preserve any aged cheese kill most harmful bacteria. Pasteurization for fluid milk that will be drunk fresh has been the rule all over the world for a century. Raw milk, with its superior flavor, has been the rule for cheese aged more than two months.

With industrialization, and especially after World War II, America left raw milk in the backward, rural past. In 1998, an industrial trade group proposed that all U.S. cheese, fresh and aged, be defined by law as beginning with pasteurized milk. This makes perfect sense for a cheese factory, which produces tens of thousands of pounds of cheese a day and combines tanks of milk from dozens of dairies. It makes no sense for an individual cheese maker who works with milk from his or her own small herd of cows, sheep, or goats and whose goal is to produce the best cheese possible. Pasteurization equipment is very expensive, and is unnecessary if the dairy follows sensible sanitation guidelines.

Cindy and David Major are important members of a small but growing band of American artisans opposing any ban on raw milk. They've joined the battle in the most effective way they know: making a sheep's milk cheese to rival any Sardinian pecorino or Lacaune *brebis*, and teaching other farmers how to do it, too. Their efforts are on a smaller scale than Roberto Rubino's but they closely mirror his, down to ripening the cheeses of many farmers in one carefully built room. And the Majors have pioneered, on their own, the idea of a Slow Food Presidium, giving instruction and marketing help to artisans who would otherwise be unable to practice their craft.

The Majors may be unusually attractive and Major Farm unusually beautiful, but the difficulties they faced in trying to keep a farm alive and make a traditional food with integrity are

typical of artisans everywhere—and especially in a country that has not valued Slow ways.

After studying international development at Harvard, Major, whose fine, almost delicate features are only accentuated by the ruddy effects of Vermont wind and winter rain, returned to his parents' farm in 1983. He had grown up helping tend and shear sheep, and now he wanted to find a way to make the farm pay for itself, something it had never done; his father sold real estate to support it. He also wanted to help imperiled neighboring farms. He took a job at a woolen mill in Putney. But his salary there, and shearing and slaughtering on the farm, were not enough.

Cindy Schwartz, who has the poignant face and long brown curls of a Van Eyck angel, learned about processing and selling milk, yogurt, and cheese at her father's dairy business in Queens, New York. Soon after she began attending a Vermont college, she met David at a contra dance. They married and settled at David's farm. Cindy's father was the one who made the outlandish suggestion that the Majors milk their sheep. In Vermont, sheep were for wool and meat. The breeds that thrived in its climate produced relatively small amounts of milk. But, as with Podolico cows in Italy, that milk was full of flavor, and could make great cheese.

Thinking something can be great is a long way from making it great, especially if you're working in an absence of traditions that could point the way and have to invent your own—the situation in which most American food artisans find themselves. For a number of years, Cindy tried making one style of cheese after another, with dismal results. "The Gouda wasn't good," she says, "and the bleu wouldn't turn blue. I buried a lot of cheese in the manure pile."

These were the wrong kinds of cheese. Cindy hadn't talked with Rubino, of course, to have the benefit of his motto: Read the Landscape.

She did pour out her heart in a letter to another wise man of cheese, Patrick Rance, the late godfather of the revival of farmhouse cheeses in England and the author of definitive guides. Rance wrote back and advised her to visit the Pyrenees, where geographic, climatic, and possibly economic conditions were similar to the ones she had described.

Using a French-speaking student who had lived with them for a summer as a translator, and Rance's *The French Cheese Book* (Macmillan) as an address book, the couple went to France in 1992. They packed a rented car with their two small children, samples of maple syrup from the sugar house on Major Farm, photographs of the farm and their sheep, and bits of experimental cheese. "The French people were so warm and receptive," Cindy says. "They really wanted to teach us how to do it right." This might have been because they tasted her samples. "How threatening can two people be," she asks, "with little kids and bad cheese?"

Generosity is typical of the story of artisans everywhere, who face similar challenges and believe that the least they can do is help others. Following the detailed advice she received in France, Cindy started making a cut-curd, natural-rind cheese aged for four months. The process of cutting curds with wires into neat little cubes and stacking them into circular forms is the one used to make Cheddar and other English farmhouse cheeses. A natural rind means that rather than being inoculated with a specific mold, the cheese is aged under controlled conditions, so protective, flavor-giving white molds form; it is brushed daily, so undesirable molds do not.

The next year, Cindy decided she was ready to enter the premier competition of U.S. artisanal cheeses, at the annual conference of the American Cheese Society—something she had never before dared to do. She chose the darkest and ugliest of her first group of just-ripened rounds from which to take a sample, so as not to jinx things. "Oh my gosh," she says, recalling her first mouthful. "It tasted so rich, creamy, and sweet. I just knew we'd finally figured it out." Vermont Shepherd received the society's blue ribbon, and Major Farm couldn't fill all its orders.

A string of awards has helped the couple spread their gospel. In 2000, the American Cheese Society gave Vermont Shepherd its best-of-show award; it had already given them its award for best farmhouse cheese in five out of seven years.

The Majors viewed their inability to meet the demand as a chance to help fellow farmers. With grants from the state agricultural department and the Vermont Land Trust, they set up a teaching center to show neighboring sheep farmers how to make cheese. Again similar to Rubino in southern Italy, they built a ripening "cave"—actually a closed cheese-storage room with controlled temperature and humidity—where the cheese would all be aged. This would be the domain of Cindy and their assistant Charlie Parent.

Five farms within a thirty-five-mile radius of Major Farm now make cheese three times a week using the Majors' recipe. The Majors regularly send technical advisers to the five other farms during production season. The farms deliver seven-day-old rounds to the cave, where Cindy, Charlie, and helpers (apprentice cheese makers—Cindy's way of passing on the generosity her French hosts showed her) brush them daily. After four months, a panel of three rates each of the cheeses; only the highest-scoring ones are sold as Vermont Shepherd. Slightly lower-scoring cheeses are sold under the name Shepherd's Tomme, and the remainder go to the manure pile. The system is based on one used by L'Etivaz, a Swiss mountain cooperative that makes Gruyère. It's another example of American artisans borrowing traditions.

Each round of cheese from each farm tastes different—proof of Rubino's point that the grass makes the cheese, and proof of Carlo Petrini's point that helpful microbes floating through the air create different flavors everywhere. Some of the Vermont Shepherd wheels are mushroomy and earthy. Some are much more aggressively flavored and salty than the mild, creamy cheese that made Vermont Shepherd's name. All are worth eating.

The Majors have added two kinds of cow's milk cheese to their repertory, so that neighboring farms can make cheese during the six months that sheep stay indoors and can't graze: a French-style *tomme*, creamy-textured and a bit tangy, and Timson, something like a Camembert, with a golden, buttery paste and a brown-orange "washed" rind. These cheeses are works in progress, continuing collaborations with other farmers and ways for them all to thrive and learn—and they all use raw milk.

The Majors exemplify the Slow Food battle plan: Think global, fight local. Help your neighbor. Make something that tastes so good that anyone who takes a bite will join the struggle.

Torsten Kramer is a big man given to big pronouncements, used to commanding without contradiction. He is a ninth-generation butcher, producing a full range of sausages, wursts, and smoked and fresh meats. His recipes and where he makes them are as authentic as is imaginable. Kramer lives and works in Lübeck, a town on the Baltic in the far north of Germany, where people think you can't

**MEAT**
*Torsten Kramer*
**GERMANY**

eat cabbage and kale without sausage, and his products are not an occasional indulgence but an everyday necessity. Kramer is the ideal Slow Food artisan, in using and reviving old recipes for products traditionally made in his region and taking care to make them from animals raised with respect. He is also a careful businessman who insists on quality but does not let the costs of producing it run away with him—another important part of the Slow Food ideal.

Even if his curt courtesy and always-busy demeanor hark back to generations past, Kramer is working in a way very different from both his forebears and his colleagues. He is a butcher in a country that has always cared about the soundness of its food supply, and that has gone through several serious mad-cow disease scares. He is younger, part of the generation that was and remains affected by the social movements of the '60s. And he's a, well, unusual fellow. You never know how he'll greet you when you walk into the 1960s mini–supermarket his father built in front of the butchering workshop. He'll tell you if he thinks you asked a dumb question. But he's also generous (and frequently quite

friendly) in explaining why his sausages and cured meats are better—the purity of the organically raised animals, the care and tradition in the preparation—and in giving out tastes.

Not that he tastes much himself. After he married a woman he met in Jordan, Kramer converted from Lutheranism to Islam. He can no longer eat most of the products he makes, because most contain pork. Instead he relies on the smell and touch that guided him through many years of apprenticeship—skills that have made him as busy and sought after as he is ornery.

It's a shame he can't enjoy his dozens of sausages and hams. They're homemade and genuine and use impeccable ingredients, which is reassuring news to anyone who grew up being told not to inquire too closely as to what went into the sausage. They're also extremely good. One bite of a wiener, for instance, shows why children who visit his store clamor for half a frank, the way their American counterparts insist their mothers buy a Tootsie Roll. The precooked sausages, moist and soft and only lightly seasoned, are made from fresh, organically raised pork, in contrast to beefy American hot dogs, which are laced with additives and soy flour and, although also precooked, good only when warmed up. Kramer's roast pork shoulder is a similar revelation—pure and sweet and barely salted, just grainy enough to give interest, and a beautiful light pink. His home-smoked ham shows you why *schinken* is sacred to all of Germany. Its rich mahogany makes prosciutto look pallid, and the flavor of the resilient meat seems to stay forever in the mouth, the husky smokiness lingering long after you swallow. Then there's the salami, cured for months and authoritatively seasoned: one with paprika, garlic, and red wine; one with cardamom and rum; one with just salt and white pepper; one with nutmeg and caraway seeds. All are light

pink flecked with ivory-colored circles of fat, like red Italian marble. All taste only of the honest ingredients in them—and the history and skill behind them.

The medieval city of Lübeck, with its corbel-roofed brick warehouses out of a Vermeer cityscape, happens to be a Slow Food redoubt. One of the first founders of a chapter outside Italy was Lothar Tubbesing, a charismatic and dedicated local restaurateur. With his wife, Heike, Tubbesing cooks and serves meals at Lachswehr, their elegant restaurant in a mansion on a city canal. Tubbesing has become a point of reference for many Europeans looking to understand how they can fit into the Slow Food movement. He has inspired other Germans and friends from Nordic countries to begin Slow Food chapters. Tubbesing has also become something of a legend at Slow Food headquarters in Italy for his exuberant dedication and for being a wellspring of ideas.

Lothar tells any Slow-minded visitor to Lübeck, which draws many tourists for its beauty and its marzipan, that it's essential to visit his friend Torsten to see an artisan with real passion for preserving local history and food. Tubbesing

is as outgoing as Kramer is recalcitrant, and when he directs people to what might be the best sausage shop in a sausage-crazed country, he makes sure to prepare them for a character.

Humanity seems to come as a vague disappointment to Kramer, who works so hard to bring it the very best and most healthful foods he can. He speaks with scorn of people who "buy with their eyes, not their brain." Take the salami he worked years to perfect without saltpeter, the nitrate that makes sausages red or rosy pink. Saltpeter makes salami attractive to the eye, and nearly every maker—certainly industrial meatpackers but most artisans, too—uses large amounts of preservatives. So reliant on saltpeter are butchers today that the art of making sausage without it has practically been lost. The trouble is the color. Kramer always gives customers who ask for salami a taste of each kind: the admittedly grayish brown one made without saltpeter, and the bright reddish orange one made with it. People don't taste or buy with their eyes shut, though, and a large number of customers automatically choose the red one.

Customers come from thirty miles away to buy Kramer's meats and sausages, because they know they can trust his products. Long before

health concerns roused the German public into demanding to know the source of its meat, Kramer decided to use only animals from local farms, most of them organically raised. During the mad-cow and foot-and-mouth scares in November 2000 and the summer of 2001 he was nearly overwhelmed by the stampede of customers to his shop—one of the few places in the united country where people could safely satisfy their cravings for sausage, a national staple. In the weeks after the first cases of mad-cow disease were discovered in Germany, his number of customers nearly tripled.

Kramer was ready for them, but not for so many. The huge increase in demand would please most businessmen, but Kramer didn't have a way of obtaining enough organically raised animals from the several farms who supplied him. And even if he could get the meat, he didn't have room to expand his production. He waited for the rush to subside, and made plans to enlarge his workrooms.

The solution, he thinks, is for there to be more artisans like him. In the kind of collaboration that happens when like-minded people find one another through Slow Food, Kramer and Tubbesing and a woman nearby who raises organic cattle have started thinking of how to sell organic food direct to customers rather than having to deal with middlemen. Tubbesing is also trying to start an outdoor, year-round market for organic farmers and artisanal producers.

Another encouraging development has taken form just a few miles from Kramer's shop: the opening in 2001 of a government-funded research center on a beautiful farm built by a local aristocrat as a hunting retreat. Its mandate is to conduct long-term studies on organically raised produce and animals. The center's establishment owes much to Renate Kunast, who was appointed Germany's minister of agriculture in the same year. Upon her appointment, Kunast called for 20 percent of the country's land to be farmed organically by the year 2010—an ambitious goal, given that perhaps 2 percent of the land and 1 percent of the farms in the entire European Union were farmed organically at the time. The rest of Europe took note.

The first task the center faced when it opened was to persuade the neighbors—that is, local politicians—that organic food doesn't mean old, wilted, gnarled, unappealing food. This perception dogs the organic movement worldwide, and the best way to counter it anywhere is to give people good organic food. For the new research station's first event, it looked for the local artisan whose products could win people over.

That artisan was Torsten Kramer. He set up a barbecue to grill a few sausages and serve some organic potato salad, another sacred national dish. Children, naturally, and skeptical local politicians too lined up in the courtyard of the picturesque former stables, at a daylong festival that brought together Lübeck Slow Food members, local farmers, and people who never thought they'd want anything organic. They came back for seconds. It helped that there was an organic version on tap of perhaps the single most-loved German food after sausage: beer. With foods like this, Germany and its neighbors might convert to organic farming sooner than anyone dared hope.

Dietrich's Meats & Country Store is near Krumsville, just off a main highway that runs through Pennsylvania Dutch country. A drive there from Philadelphia, an hour or so away, passes through fertile farmland on roads lined with beautiful stone barns. Dietrich's is large and modern, with many kinds of locally made hard pretzels in racks near the door, and a glass case full of fresh meats and sausages running the length of the back wall. Jars of apple butter, home-fermented sauerkraut, and various pickled meats cover the counter, and beside the cash register are homemade crumb-topped shoofly pies, marbled "funny cakes," domed yeast breads, and lemon meringue pies. At Dietrich's and the farms around it, farming and butchering survive little changed from a century ago.

People come from many states to find the owner, Verna Dietrich. They know they can trust her meat, and they know how good her sausages are. The similarities to Torsten Kramer are many: they both draw on the same German traditions (for much of America's history, over half its population was of German descent), they both draw people from afar for the integrity of their meats, and they're both outsized characters.

Verna Dietrich is descended from a long line of Pennsylvania Dutch farmers, and is the mistress of a wealth of traditional cuts and preparations. She grew up on a dairy farm in Virginville, a town nine miles south of Krumsville. All the recipes for the ninety or so meat products she now stocks came from her own family, she says, chiefly from a grandmother with whom she lived for ten years of her childhood. These recipes are extremely close to the ones Kramer uses in Germany: the traditions he preserves are the same ones that inspired her ancestors.

"Huge in size and opinions," the historian William Woys Weaver, an authority on Pennsylvania Dutch food and culture, calls Dietrich, and anyone entering the store can verify his description. Her wide, ringleted head bobs behind the counter, and her large aproned form comes into view when she emerges to find an item for a customer. She never stops surveying her store to make sure customers either find what they want or want something.

The animals Dietrich uses are not organically raised, but the Mennonites who own the farms from which she buys them use traditional ways of feeding and raising animals. These

**MEAT**
*Verna Dietrich*
**PENNSYLVANIA**

involve few drugs, and as much time outdoors as possible. She also raises many animals herself, or rather her family does. Verna's husband, Willard, helped by one of their three sons, Glenn, raises enough pigs, lambs, and cattle to supply the store—quite a lot of animals, given that Dietrich's is open seven days a week, handles an extensive mail-order business, and operates a booth every Friday and Saturday at Renninger's farmers' market, in Kutztown, the tourist capital of Pennsylvania Dutch country. Every Tuesday the family slaughters about twenty pigs, three or four lambs, and four or five cattle. Marlin, another son, works in the store, in the meat-cutting and sausage-making room in the back; his wife, Dawn, helps keep the books. The kitchen, a separate room, is frequently suffused with the smell of a deep kettle of hot lard, in which Debbie Dietrich, another daughter-in-law, fries *Fastnachts*, square Lenten doughnuts made from a yeast dough containing mashed potatoes, butter, and lard.

"You won't find many places that slaughter their own pork, beef, and lamb and do their own processing," Dietrich says. "We make everything here." She doesn't stop for breath as she recites her products like a country auctioneer, keeping an eye on the customers and occasionally addressing them mid-spiel: "Corn beef fresh and smoked, fresh and smoked sausages, Lebanon and sweet bologna, German mince bologna, ducks, geese, pheasant, quail, chukar—that's partridge—guinea hens, goat, lamb, smoked ducks, turkeys, capons, rabbits, we raise our own rabbits. Can I help you? We have everything head to tail—brains and sweetbreads, oxtail, hearts, tongues, kidneys. We can our own tripe, pig's feet, and souse. We cure our own Westphalian hams, old-fashioned farmers' and mild-cured hams, double-smoked bacon and regular hickory smoked, beef bacon, Canadian bacon, beef jerky, slim jims hot—mild, or sweet—hot dogs and German wieners. Bratwurst and veal bratwurst, knackwurst, ring bolognas—they're all beef, you eat them for a snack like kielbasa—and cheese ring bologna with pieces of cheese that melt when you cook it, and a full line of German products like *Mettwurst* and *Jagdwurst*. Are you looking for anything special?"

Dietrich slips favored customers little tastes of products in addition to the copious array of tiny cubes of salamis and sausages always immediately set out on sample trays: liverwurst you want to spread on German rye bread; Lebanon bologna, a salami emblematic of the Pennsylvania Dutch larder and named for the county where it was first commercially produced. What characterizes Lebanon bologna is the use of beef rather than pork, a distinct sweetness, and a gentle spicing with hints of ginger, paprika, mustard, and mace. It's so good you want a steady supply. Luckily, Dietrich ships all her cooked meats anywhere in the country.

These are matchless components of the American larder—ones at risk of disappearing, and ones Slow Food USA will put its resources behind to make sure they don't vanish. America has been fortunate in being spared the panics and destruction of animal diseases that brought change to Europe, change that drew many Europeans to the Slow Food movement and led governments to take organic farming seriously at last. Until the U.S. government funds the kind of research center the German government has set up near Kramer's sausage shop, Americans looking for the kind of wholesome, traditional meat his customers drive so far to get will have to mail-order Dietrich's dozens of sausages and smoked meats. Or they can drive to visit the proprietress herself. That's an adventure in itself.

I n the relentless late-summer heat of the Algarve, on the southern coast of Portugal, shirtless young men bent over shallow rectangular pools of seawater dense with salt use wooden rakes to draw the wet white salt to the side. The long, pyramid-shaped salt piles that build up look like miniature alpine peaks on a blinding winter's day. It's a disorienting image on a sunbeaten morning.

**SALT**

*João Navalho*

**PORTUGAL**

After a siesta, the young men return to the small salt pans, laid out in a winding patchwork following the line of a tidal marsh area a few miles from the Atlantic. They have exchanged their flat-bottomed rakes for long-handled skimmers that look something like butterfly nets. Again they bend over the water, looking for irregularly shaped gossamer formations that skitter along the top—visible only if you catch them at the right angle, glinting in the sun.

This is *fleur de sel,* or *flor de sal* to the Portuguese. It's the cream of the salt pan, the newly formed crystals that float on the surface before becoming big and heavy enough to fall to the bottom. The micalike formations must be harvested quickly, within hours of forming, before they fall. *Fleur de sel* is a legend in the world of gourmet salt—a rare, almost unfindable, extremely expensive legend. The content and health benefits of *fleur de sel* and the hand-harvested traditional sea salt that the young men raked in the morning—itself rare in an age of bland, mechanically harvested sea salt—are identical. What's different is the texture. *Fleur de sel* crumbles at a touch and melts on the tongue.

It has a vibrant, full, almost sweet flavor that's a world removed from purified salt.

The *fleur de sel* that has recently excited chefs and gourmets in many countries is something French chefs have long known about, because they got it from the coast of Brittany. *Fleur de sel* has always been a luxury ingredient, to be sprinkled over a dish at the very last minute—before it can dissolve into the *sauce madère* or the *filet à poele,* so the diner can have the pleasure of the slight crackle between the teeth and then the quick, delicious melting on the tongue.

Only in the 1990s did a salt-harvesting cooperative in Guérande, in Brittany, begin to export little bags of *fleur de sel* to retail to gourmet shops as a boutique item. Demand for its unique flavor and especially its texture almost immediately outstripped supply. Few people willing to pay a royal sum for it know that a beautiful, and many would say superior, version is being sold in Portugal at a fraction of the price.

That's because the men raking the Portuguese salt pans began doing it only at the end of the 1990s, when an idealistic group of young marine biologists took an enforced detour from their plans to make and sell algae through Necton, their newly formed company. The detour was the result of learning about the ancient history of their carefully selected site. Their new home was on a part of the Atlantic coastline long among the world's primary producers of a product man cannot live without: salt.

The knowledge of how to care for salinas, small salt pans—a whole language of terms for tools and the cycle of tending and harvesting—was being lost. *Marenotos,* salt-pan workers who grew up knowing it, were aging and disappearing as their children looked to other businesses to survive. With the salt pans and the workers went a fragile ecosystem already at risk in a heavily touristed part of Portugal.

Its unplanned role in the revival of an ancient trade won Necton a special Slow Food Award in 2001. The award will be of great help in allowing the company to do what it must: make the beautiful, pristine white, delicious, environment-conserving but labor-intensive salt pay for itself, so the idealistic group can get back to its original plans.

A driving force of Necton is the energetic João Navalho, who was born in Mozambique in 1965 of Portuguese parents and moved to Lisbon as a child. While earning a graduate degree in aquaculture, he and Vitor Verdelho, a friend studying biotechnology, won a grant to look for new ways to harness Portugal's natural resources. Portugal needed to take advantage of the Algarve's sun and sea, the graduate students thought, beyond bargain-rate planeloads of German and English tourists. These visitors didn't help the environment, and neither did the big hotels built speedily and carelessly to house them.

The students wanted to use new technology to make large quantities of algae that produce beta-carotene, which is valuable to food producers who want a healthful, nonchemical orange dye. In 1994, they began looking for a part of the coastline with maximal sunlight and plentiful clean seawater. After years of searching, they found the perfect spot: twelve hectares (about thirty acres) of salt marshes in the protected National Park of Ria Formosa, in the tidal flats near the tourist centers of Olhão and Faro. Seville is just ninety miles away, and Lisbon one-hundred-eighty. The constantly beating sun and the continual flow of seawater, free of polluting effluents from the industries that mar much of the Atlantic coastline, would be ideal for the cutting-edge technology they planned to use. A few grants and their own educations would be their capital, and they would run the company on socialist ideals: all workers, whatever their position, would be stockholders and share profits. Then the recent graduates found out about salt.

For thousands of years, salt was the reason people came to this particular part of the world. The Egyptians were probably the first civilization to evaporate seawater methodically to extract salt, and the Phoenicians probably brought their early technology to the Portuguese Atlantic coast. The presence of Roman ruins in the Algarve suggests that the Romans produced salt there, as they did on much of the coastline. By the year 1000, the Algarve was sending salt to the rest of Europe, and in the fifteenth and sixteenth centuries, the Age of Exploration, salt helped Portugal consolidate its position as a world power. A payment of salt enabled the Portuguese to regain Brazil from the Dutch.

But the countries of northern and eastern Europe learned to mine rock salt in caves, and in the mid-twentieth century, mechanization in the mines and cheap transport and better roads across the Continent made sea salt relatively expensive. Mechanization arrived for the production and harvest of sea salt, too, including in the Algarve. After World War II, the *marenotos* found they could not withstand price competition from dirt-cheap rock salt, and abandoned their work tending salinas to find jobs in factories and cities. Portuguese sea salt, even if mechanically harvested, maintained its high reputation: large conglomerates sell Portuguese sea salt to the French, for table use, and ship inferior salt back to Portugal. But the small salt pans that had kept alive local economies and agricultural artisans vanished.

Navalho and his coworkers were upset to find that small salt pans on their own and adjoining property had been abandoned to become communal dumping grounds. The only businesses they saw around them were standard fish farms and huge salt pans regulated by computers and harvested annually by machines with almost no help from workmen. (Private land ownership is allowed within the large national park, as long as it is for nonpolluting agricultural use.) The rest, the honeycomb of small

rectangular salt pans that followed the sluices of the intertidal shores, were falling out of use.

"The place was like a desert," Navalho tells visitors touring Necton. "I like to see flamingos and birds. If you don't fill the pans with water every year and you're not taking care of them every day, they'll be dirty, dry, and ugly. And the birds will be gone—not just flamingos but avocets, plovers, egrets, dozens of others."

The collaborators faced an urgent, and large, change of plan. Their first commitment was to the environment. That meant keeping the wetlands—a rare survival in a highly populated region of the world's most productive ecosystem after rain forests—wet. They already employed a *marenoto,* Maximino Guerreiro, to take care of the industrial-sized salt pan on Necton's property. Guerreiro, who grew up tending small salinas, warned the new owners that they'd better take care of the smaller pans, too, if they didn't want them to turn into dumps. Besides, he said, the salt from the smaller salinas—harvested several times over

the summer rather than once at the end, ahead of the fall rains—tasted much better and was much healthier, too. He could find the tools, and show young apprentices how it was done.

Through the spring and summer of 1998, the year after Necton began, the regular Necton workers tended the pans. They were helped by a few young men Guerreiro trained during the busy salt harvest, which happens every five to seven weeks, depending on the heat of the sun and the force of the drying north winds. At summer's end, Necton had a crop of dazzlingly white salt.

The young directors were thrilled. They had made a magnificent product. Then they tried to sell it, and quickly realized why they saw so much trash instead of salt on their way to and from work.

According to Portuguese law, Necton can't even sell its salt for the table. In 1973, the government set new standards defining three categories of salt. The highest was pure sodium chloride, the product that industry wants. Sodium chloride is a primary ingredient in the making of glass, paints, batteries, explosives, and glues; plastics makers need it for polyvinylchloride (PVC), the polymer in plastic wrap and many other products. It is also the salt most people buy for the table. Additives such as iodine and fluoride are allowed for table salt, as are the anticaking agents potassium cyanide and aluminum silicate. The second category is 96 percent sodium chloride, and the third is anything below 96 percent—fit only for trucks to dump onto the road, not for the table. This seeming last choice is really the first: the world's chief use of salt is to prevent freezing.

Necton's salt, incredibly, falls into this third category. Hand-harvested, sun-dried sea salt has a far greater variety of mineral salts than plain, purified sodium chloride. Some of these mineral salts, like magnesium, iron, and calcium, are particularly good for health, and occur in high quantity in unpurified sea salt. Unprocessed sea salt also contains many micronutrients that are washed out of mechanical salt along with all the other impurities that machines introduce. But Portuguese authorities consider unwashed, unpurified sea salt to be unfit for human consumption. The best Necton could do that first year was to sell its salt at the same price as the mechanically harvested crop from their one large salt pan—even though the hand-harvested salt required ten times as much labor. The mixed salt would be washed and "purified" in a processing plant.

Necton found a way around its status problems through the guidance of a neighboring natural reserve where another *marenoto* was still producing traditional sea salt. An administrator of the reserve brought together a few *marenotos* in a group called TradiSal, and helped several of its ten members obtain what is likely the world's only certification of unrefined organic sea salt. The certificate, issued by a French group called Nature et Progrès, guarantees that salt has been found free of eighty-two possible contaminants, including pesticides, radioactivity, various bacteria, and the heavy metals that often appear in trace quantities in industrial salt because of the machinery that rolls across salt beds. For Necton, winning the certification has the extra benefit of demonstrating that the algae it plans to sell will be produced in a pure environment.

But it won't change antiquated Portuguese law. TradiSal is petitioning Lisbon to exclude two categories from the restrictions of the infamous third class: traditional sea salt and *flor de sal*. It also wants to create an internationally recognized logo that will appear on each bag of salt, and to create a market that will appreciate, and pay for, it.

"We don't want to be the salt kings," Navalho says. Necton just wants to preserve an endangered tradition and the endangered environment that goes along with it, before turning back to its real work—making algae.

Michael O'Leary throws a rust-red crab into an orange plastic laundry basket in his just-for-business small fishing boat. The red-bearded fisherman closes the slatted boxlike trap from which he took the crab and, with a decisive flick, throws it back into the water. Standing behind the wheel in a pilot's cabin, the grizzled, tattooed skipper heads for the next trap, idling the engine when he comes close. O'Leary clamps a big hook hanging from a pulley onto the line the skipper has been following, and sets the pulley's motor running. The next trap appears from the deep, pulled up the pulley's rope fast, like a phantasm heading at you in a science-fiction movie. O'Leary steadies it on the ledge of the gunwale and sticks his wet, muddy, cotton-gloved hand into the top to pull out three angry crabs. He tosses them into the basket with a practiced and satisfied motion and turns to the visiting passengers admiring the quaint village and beautiful beaches just a few hundred feet away. "I know y'all didn't come out here to do this all day," he says. "It ain't *that* fun."

Most visitors come to O'Leary's part of the world, Longboat Key, on Florida's western Gulf Coast, strictly to have fun. It's one of the most expensive parts of a very expensive coastline. But a few people work, too, and not just in the condominium complexes, hotels, tennis courts, and golf courses that have taken over every buildable square foot on the long, narrow strip of land connected by bridge to the city of Sarasota. O'Leary makes his living catching one of the country's rarest and best-tasting delicacies from the sea: stone crabs.

North America has several crustaceans to call its own, wild, hard-shelled, elusive swimmers with meat so good that food lovers travel hundreds or even thousands of miles to taste them fresh and on-site. The best known, of course, is *Homarus americanus,* usually called Maine lobster

but just as common off the Canadian Atlantic coast. Norway lobster, usually called scampi and fished in cold northeast Atlantic waters, is the second most prized, even if most people mistake it for giant shrimp (Italian restaurants in America often serve shrimp as scampi).

Stone crabs, the third most valuable crustacean, have a following as fanatical as lobster's. Stone crabs are a curious breed. Only their claws

SHELLFISH
*Michael O'Leary*
FLORIDA

are harvested, and their meat is uniquely dense and rich. The only places in the world stone crabs live are the Gulf Coast, as far west as Texas and Louisiana, and the Atlantic coast, as far north as South Carolina. Their Garbo-like appearances and limited season make them a highlight and a reason for winter vacations, just as people look forward to summer holidays in Maine as much for the lobster as for the fir trees and rocky coastline.

The blue crab is an object of veneration in Baltimore, where wielding a wooden mallet to crack one big reddish-brown creature after another on a picnic table covered with sturdy brown paper is among America's greatest treats. The sweet, fibrous meat of Maryland blue crab is flavored with the seawater that generously permeates it; diners taste the tang of salt against the bay leaf and hit of hot red pepper every cook adds to the boiling water. Although "beautiful swimmers," as the Latin name of blue crabs has them, are in their full glory in the Chesapeake Bay, they are plentiful up and down the Eastern seaboard, and are the species that forms most people's idea of how crabmeat should taste.

The flesh of stone crab claws, their close relatives, is far firmer—meaty, in fact, by comparison with the deliciously fugitive threads of blue crab that diners pick deep out of shells. Most people compare the meat of stone crabs with lobster. Even if someone who lives near Maine will never find it quite as fully flavored or distinctive, its flavor does span both worlds. Any crab or lobster lover can develop a serious stone crab addiction on a visit to Florida.

A few dozen relatively large-scale fishermen along the state's Gulf Coast bring in thousands of pounds of stone crabs each season, but catching the crabs is still mostly the purview of small entrepreneurs like O'Leary—fishermen who work long, hard days with just enough help to lay and pull traps. They own their own boats and pay insurance and labor costs themselves. Luckily, there are large numbers of people hungry for stone crab, and so the market is assured. And, to a greater degree than with most wild seafood, the catch is assured as well. Foresighted laws passed by the Florida state legislature in the

1970s have helped preserve the population and keep up the stock.

Even the most tenderhearted shellfish lover can feast on stone crab claws with little guilt, because the crab grows itself another claw and hardly notices the loss. An adult crab can regenerate claws, as it continually grows new shells during its frequent molting. Attempts to farm stone crabs have failed; stocks continue to hold steady thanks to the careful management of a native species. The claw must be neatly snapped off at the right place, making a clean break that closes immediately. This is achieved by either an expert twisting motion of the fisherman's wrist or by puncturing the claw joint with a sharp probe in just the right place, forcing the crab to contract its muscles and cleanly shed its claw.

"I should have a name for some of these crabs," O'Leary says, as he snaps off a claw. "I've handled them more than once." Florida law specifies the length a claw must have reached before it may be taken, to ensure the best

chance of regrowth, and dictates that any egg-bearing female be thrown back unmolested. Declawed or not, every crab must be immediately returned to the water, or held in a shaded place and wetted down every half hour before being thrown back. It is illegal for fishermen to possess a whole stone crab, dead or alive, and illegal to fish at night. To safeguard the breeding cycle, fishing is forbidden outside the season, which runs from October 15 to May 15. Stone crabs, already a limited species, have thus been preserved.

Each fisherman lays his traps—as many as four hundred—five days before the season begins, the first date it is legal to do so. This work can legally be done at night, and most fishermen take advantage of darkness to stake out the patch of ocean they think will yield the most crabs. They attach their traps to a line they lay northwest to southeast, so that should a storm blow up they can retreat quickly. Stone crabs are unpredictable, even whimsical, in their movements, and traps that are nearly empty one day can

hold six or seven crabs apiece—a very healthy number, fishermen say—just three or four days later. With an extra man or two and a skipper, a fisherman with a boat the modest size of O'Leary's can pull one hundred traps an hour.

The rhythm is fast, the clatter of the traps against the side of the boat and the slap as O'Leary throws the still-tethered traps back into the drink propulsive. When the laundry basket is full of crabs, and a shallow box beside it is nearly covered with grouper, chum, and other small fish to be used as bait next time, O'Leary and his skipper decide to go back in. This is when O'Leary gets busy removing the claws and throwing back the rest of the crabs in a sure, steady stream as the boat speeds for home, almost as if the creatures, still alive and vigorously kicking, were cherry pits or apple cores.

O'Leary brings his catch to an unchanged piece of Americana—the sort of place any Slow Food member goes out of the way to visit: Moore's Stone Crab Restaurant. The stone crab business still has a kind of cozy familiarity rare in the United States. The fishermen and wholesalers who stake their survival on the survival of the stone crab all know one another. Moore's goes through 200,000 pounds of claws a year. This is just a third of what the most famous Florida purveyor, Joe's Stone Crab, in Miami, goes through, and a fraction of the average annual Florida haul of about 3.5 million pounds. But it is not a negligible fraction.

In an age of fast food, Moore's is one of those family-run shorefront restaurants that hardly exist anymore, a place where everyone lines up at the screen door on the wide wooden verandah and walks down to the water while waiting for their name to be called. It's also a part of what remains of Longboat Key as it was before rich retirees and tourists drove out working people. Until recently, this end of the key, farthest from Sarasota, was mainly a fishing village, a year-round community where working people could afford to live. Today its scenic little houses have tastefully applied gingerbread and newly restored wood where not long ago there was economical aluminum siding. But even they are on their way to ostentatious gentility, as not-from-here settlers buy them up and renovate.

The heart of Moore's operation is a square concrete-floored room behind the kitchen, with a big walk-in refrigerator set off only by long plastic flaps. This is the room that O'Leary and other fishermen who sell their catch exclusively to Moore's call when they have finished pulling traps for the day, to say, "Fire up the kettle."

When the boat arrives at the Moore's dock, a worker greets it and helps carry in the crate of claws.

The kettle is indeed boiling, but this is far from an ordinary pot. It's a stainless-steel industrial-sized kettle, big as a hot tub. A wire basket nearly the size of the kettle is suspended over the boiling water, held by a pulley, waiting for the day's catch. The basket of mottled brown claws is lowered on its hook into the water, where the crabs are steamed for eighteen minutes. The winch pulls the now bright red crabs from the kettle, and they trundle several feet over a large, rectangular stainless-steel vat of ice. A jerk of the rope tilts the basket and dumps the cooked crabs into the ice bath. The quantity of ice is huge, to comply with the guidelines of HACCP (Hazard Analysis and Critical Control Point), the international food-safety code that requires cooked crabs to be thoroughly chilled for four minutes after coming out of their steam bath. The chilled crabs then go into boxes in the walk-in refrigerator, to be served in the restaurant or packed for shipping.

Paper menu placemats show Moore's endearingly clumsy logo of a bright red stone crab. The specialty, of course, is boiled and chilled claws, served on oval plates with tartar sauce and a wedge of iceberg lettuce. Some things are better left perfectly plain. Stone crab claws—thick, cool, popping with seawater, requiring just enough cracking and picking to be a challenge amply rewarded—meet that test of perfect simplicity.

Picking and crushing the grapes for ice wine—the sweetest, most intense concentration of grape flavor in a bottle—is something out of a folk tale. The grapes must be picked on several of the coldest nights of the year, preferably by moonlight, and pressed outdoors before the rising sun can begin to melt them. Ice wine is one of the most peculiar, troublesome wines in the world to make. It also occupies a niche where the New World can successfully compete with the Old, by capitalizing on local climates and native grapes instead of fighting them.

Canada has lately taken to ice wine the way Napa and Sonoma did to Cabernet, and for the same reason: ice wine has brought international prizes and big increases in sales to the Canadian wine industry, which, like California's, labored for decades with little recognition. Canadian wine makers have reanimated a wine that had practically disappeared in its northern European birthplace. And they have done this without denaturing it, as attempts to re-create foods and wines far from their homes often do.

This is Slow Food philosophy in action: giving new life to a product that requires so much care and handwork that it has almost been forgotten. The twist here is awakening a Sleeping Beauty on another continent. The Princes Charming in this story were all, as it happens, from its native land. One more twist: the evil queen transformed herself into a big, black flock of starlings.

Efforts to make drinkable wine in America were vexed from the start. Thomas Jefferson famously failed to coax European grapes into thriving at Monticello. Early explorers of the Americas carried many New World fruits and vegetables to Europe with such success that centuries later settlers imported them back to their native land (think of the tomato and the potato). But grapes were different. Jefferson and others who hoped to make wine in the colonies dismissed as "foxy" the musty scent of native varieties such as Concord and Catawba, familiar to schoolchildren as the flavor of grape jelly and to teenagers sneaking Manischewitz and Cold Duck.

Only after the late nineteenth century, when Italian immigrants recognized that European wine grapes could thrive in the Mediterranean-

WINE
*Karl Kaiser*
CANADA

like climate of northern California, and only after their descendants decided to go head-to-head with the great wine makers of France and Italy, did the wine world take the New World seriously. Another group of immigrants—Germans and Austrians in Ontario—saw decades later that they, too, could turn a climate similar to the one they had left behind to their advantage.

The Niagara Peninsula, which runs along Lake Ontario a few miles north of the U.S. border, is suited to cool-climate grapes. The lake stores summer heat and releases it into the cooling autumn air, permitting long ripening. It was here that a series of French hybrid grapes, so called because French viticulturists crossed southern European varieties with native American ones that could withstand disease and the cold, were developed at the turn of the twentieth century. White grapes proved more successful than red. The most highly adaptable white variety was Vidal, a cross including the popular wine grape known in Italy as Trebbiano and in France as Ugni Blanc. Vidal grapes are relatively high in acidity, a characteristic of most cool-climate white grapes and a quality needed to balance the sweetness of ice wine. They also have extremely tough skins, another necessity if they are to survive the cycle of freezing and thawing necessary for ice wine grapes.

Several wine makers on the peninsula, each with a German or Austrian background, decided in the early 1980s that they were growing the right grapes and working in just the right conditions to produce ice wine. Maybe they could make a product to rival that of their homelands. Maybe they could make a better one. For a while they talked about the possibility, almost as a joke—something to do if the seemingly endless work in their young wineries ever left them any time. In 1983, they decided to leave a few rows of Vidal and Riesling vines unpicked in each of their vineyards and see them through several hard frosts. The harvest was over by late October, as usual, and the first hard frosts were due in early December; mild Novembers and suddenly cold Decembers are typical of the peninsula, and a good augury for ice wine. Then, on December 1, one of the wine makers lost his entire crop.

"I was in Rochester, at a wine conference," Karl Kaiser, the wine maker, still recalls with wonder and frustration. "I got back at two, and there were no grapes. I asked our vineyard fellow, 'What happened? Did you guys pick it?'" No, was the answer: starlings ate them all, in a few greedy minutes. Lesson one, then, was to net the vines soon after the October harvest.

Nine years earlier, Kaiser, a big, balding, mustachioed man with a kindly, intelligent face, had joined forces with Donald Ziraldo to open the Inniskillin Winery. Kaiser, who was exposed to wine making as a high school student in a Cistercian monastery boarding school in rural Austria, would be the wine maker; Ziraldo, born in Canada to immigrants from the Italian region of Friuli, would oversee the business and promotion. They bought a farm for the winery near Niagara-on-the-Lake, a pretty town eight miles north of Niagara Falls, and started making and selling several kinds of table wine. Ice wine

began to seem like a good way to catch the attention of a world that remained steadfastly uninterested in a newly ambitious industry.

Sweet wines are among the world's slowest, both in time and in the Slow Food sense. To make them, vintners—or, as has been traditional for hundreds of years, small farmers who tend a few vines to produce a homemade holiday treat— must somehow concentrate the grapes' sugars.

The ways of concentration are many, and the traditional ones rely on weather. In cool climates, sun and warm air won't do the job. Instead vintners hope that insects (or birds, or hail, or mildew) will bore tiny holes in the grape skins, to allow the entry of the fungus *Botrytis cinerea,* called noble rot when vintners want it and bunch rot when they don't. If conditions are just right, the botrytis will concentrate the sugars while leaving the acid intact, resulting in honeyed tropical-fruit flavors. Waiting for the right rot is a big gamble, though, and one that frequently fails to pay off. That's why German late-harvest Rieslings, with their endless names (Beerenauslese, Trockenbeerenauslese), and Sauternes (of which Château d'Yquem is the ne plus ultra) are rare and costly. It's also why they're disappearing. There's no way to hurry these wines along by using man-made bacteria or artificial climate control or machines.

The requirements for ice wine are much simpler: a couple of cold spells after a long ripening. Freeze-thaw cycles produce some of the same complexity that noble rot does, especially the overtones of peach and apricot and of tropical fruits such as mango and litchi (although not the honeyed quality, which is unique to botrytis). They also result in enormous concentration: a great deal of water is lost to the cold, dry air, and most of what remains is trapped in crystals when the grapes are picked.

The bunches go straight into the press, stems and all. What comes out are drops of syrup, the part of the grape highest in sugar and other flavors. Great force is necessary to extract

these viscous drops: even today's powerful hydraulic presses, which typically press tons of grapes in an hour, take many hours to press a ton of frozen grapes. The yield is just one-fifth of the juice that grapes harvested normally would provide.

The wine makers on the Niagara Peninsula made things up as they went along, relying on their memories of the folk experiences of their youth—something rare in today's high-technology wine world. In the first years of their experiments, for instance, they more or less guessed which night to pick the grapes. Then they became slightly more scientific. "I have a digital display thermometer in my bedroom," Klaus Reif, of the Reif Estate Winery, says.

"When it's cold enough, we call everyone. We don't do it night after night, because that's too hard on people."

At first winery workers, drawn by the novelty, volunteered for the night harvests. Then the sweet power and storybook enchantment of making ice wine caught on. Every peninsula winery began producing one, and vintners had to find a core of workers who could do a full night's work on no notice and who were prepared to dress extremely warmly, down to their (usually bare) fingertips. The allure of moonlight on snow-covered vines proved strong among Ontarians, who started ordering ice wine with dessert and made ice wine festivals popular. Now wineries are in the unexpected position of fending off civilian volunteers.

Klaus Reif sees why. "You start at midnight and work until eight," he says. "It's ten to fourteen degrees, and with the wind chill it feels like thirty below. But it's amazing. People don't talk. They work along, quiet and peaceful. Some nights there's a snow layer and a full moon, and you hardly need any light. It's an awesome feeling."

The turning point for Canadian ice wine, and perhaps for the Canadian wine industry, was the awarding of a grand prize to an Inniskillin ice wine at Vinexpo, in Bordeaux, the largest annual trade show, in 1991. No Canadian wine had ever received anything like it. Inniskillin has gone from producing sixty-six cases in 1984, its first year, to twelve thousand cases in 2000. In 1998, Ontario sold double the number of cases that Germany did.

The unexpected success of ice wine has led wine makers to try a few innovations that are probably best discarded, such as oak-aged Vidal, which tastes oddly smoky (botrytis wines benefit from wood aging, but frozen grapes don't), and ice wine made from red Cabernet Franc grapes, which tastes like mildly alcoholic grape syrup.

Vidal remains the flagship Niagara Peninsula ice wine, and wins competition after competition.

But even better ice wines exist. "I say that Vidal has lipstick," Kaiser says, half in apology. "The acidity in Riesling is much pointier." Riesling is the grape that accounts for the greatness of the wines of his and his fellow wine makers' home countries of Austria and Germany. It also makes superior ice wine. Happily, many Niagara wineries grow it. Unlike German late-harvest Rieslings, Riesling ice wine does not require botrytis (notable makers include Konzelmann, Reif, and Malivoire).

Then there is a New World revelation: sparkling ice wine. The sparkle is natural, Kaiser explains. The wine is fermented in steel tanks, not bottles, much like the lightly effervescent—and irresistible—Moscato d'Asti. Sparkling Riesling ice wine is bright and refreshing. It's by far the nicest way to persuade even the sugar-averse that ice wine is something to treasure—perhaps with an apple tart made from rare North American varieties, or all on its own as dessert in a glass. It's also a delicious example of a rediscovered wine that builds on Old World expertise with New World ingenuity.

Twenty-three years ago, an animated, kindly Frenchman named André Dubosc was about to become the director of Plaimont, a cooperative that many fellow grape growers depended on to support their families. He depended on it, too: the vineyards he inherited from his father, who had helped create Plaimont, sold all their grapes to the cooperative. Dubosc lives in one of the least-known parts of France—the Gers, a part of Gascony in the deep Southwest midway between the Atlantic and the Pyrenees and midway between the cities of Bordeaux and Toulouse. The local welcome is unusually warm and embracing in a country that often takes for granted that visitors will pay tribute to its food and wine. The food is sumptuous: foie gras, confit, anything made from fattened geese and ducks.

The wine isn't wine, it's Armagnac—distilled white wine sold at prices that rival those of the most expensive brandies, of which it is a glorious example. Local cooperatives had for decades done very nicely selling grapes that go into the base wines for Armagnac. But as Dubosc prepared to assume his responsibilities, he worried that Plaimont could become a victim of the newly international wine world. He began looking for other wines it could make, and for other grapes his fellow growers could plant. In a country that prides itself on centuries of tradition that inspire the world, this was radical thinking. It was even, heaven forbid, like something they might come up with in America.

Why tamper with a product that has been made and sold across the known world for five hundred years? Because large and established makers of Armagnac had the buying power to look beyond Plaimont. And because the agri-efficient hybrid grapes that had been planted after World War II were falling out of favor. Agricultural consultants warned the members of Plaimont that they must think seriously about taking two large steps: go back to growing grapes that had been traditional in their region; and start selling wine directly to consumers in bottles, rather than to Armagnac distillers in barrels. Otherwise, the consultants said, they risked losing everything: soil quality, the few old vines that survived, their livelihoods.

Even in places where wine has been made since ancient times, native grape varieties can fall out

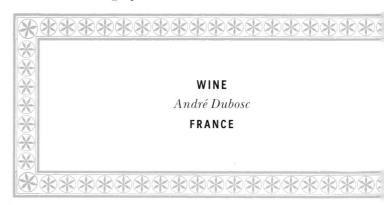

WINE

*André Dubosc*

FRANCE

of use and become endangered. Growers plant the few varieties the market seems to want, using hybrids that industrial suppliers promise will yield bumper crops with minimal effort. France itself, still the world's largest producer of wine and guardian of wine greatness, has lost large swaths of its best vineyards, which for centuries were planted with local varieties, to Merlot and other modish grapes once considered fit only for blending.

France did avoid the silliest fads (white Zinfandel, wine coolers) as other countries struggled to gain a foothold on the mountain of which France remained king. But as wine growers in other countries, especially the United States and Australia, embraced organic farming, French growers stubbornly held to the practices of their fathers, using precautionary mineral treatments and herbicides and pesticides.

It didn't take a visionary or someone dedicated to local history to heed the warning the consultants gave Plaimont. Luckily, Dubosc was both: a visionary in love with the history of his region's grapes. A wiry, silver-haired man whose face is in motion on the rare occasions when the rest of him is not, Dubosc has the gift of seeing the wider world while closely exploring the narrow one he lives in.

When the men of the tiny village of Saint-Mont, in the heart of the Gers, returned home after the war, they found the caves for aging wine in disrepair and the land badly neglected. Like many other small French wine makers returning to the same kinds of problems, they decided to band together in the kind of cooperative that was then changing the wine industry in France. They rebuilt the caves and repaired their vineyards, and erected a new central winery on the main road just below Saint-Mont. This kept alive the village's historical economy, and gave the veterans something they could pass on to their children.

The very wines those war veterans had saved looked to be at risk of losing their market, and Dubosc had to find something to pass on to the next generation. The Southwest is particularly rich in eccentric grapes—so eccentric that its wines were thought fit only to be boiled off into alcoholic fumes for brandy. The famous grapes, and famous estate bottlings, were all an hour's drive away, in Bordeaux. Yet the Southwest has its own charms and vibrant appeal, and Dubosc knew there must be a way to convey that in a bottle. The charm has a distinctly Catalan touch. You can see the Pyrenees from the top of the hill in Saint-Mont, where there is a beautiful medieval monastery church with marvelous Romanesque capitals. A Catalan sociability and the Basque mountain dweller's proud independence leaven the usual French diffidence and conservatism.

Why not take advantage of both this sociable independence and the eccentric grapes? Dubosc wondered. Perhaps some of those oddball Southwest grapes could remake the region's reputation.

Dubosc looked to a new category, *vins de pays,* that the French wine standards board had created in the 1970s to help threatened wine makers. This forward-looking initiative was a way to foster the rediscovery and revival of minor wines that had never been considered drinkable on their own. Even the name gave new respect to what had been thought inconsequential. "Wines of the country," with the implication of a specific countryside and place, certainly sounded better than *vin ordinaire* and *vin de table.*

Dubosc tried to convince the members of the Plaimont cooperative to grow old grape varieties. It took time. In the 1980s, as part of his effort, he invited scholars from the universities of Bordeaux and Montpellier, both of which specialize in wine making, to help identify varieties in the region. The grape detectives went looking in vineyard corners and people's backyards, and came up with more than forty.

One discovery, in a Plaimont member's kitchen garden, was particularly precious: a few rows of vines surviving intact from the time before the phylloxera epidemic of the 1870s and 1880s, which decimated the European wine industry. It was American rootstock that rescued the industry then. Dubosc's dream is that in the event of another crisis, disease-resistant French rootstock will save the day. And he is still awaiting proof of his pet theory—that, contrary to the history books, the odd local grapes, which suit the cool Atlantic climate much better than Mediterranean varieties, came not by sea with Phoenician and Roman conquerors but across the Pyrenees with the Basques.

Dubosc worked with wine makers to plant and develop new *vins de pays,* blends assembled from local grapes that hadn't been grown commercially for generations. He convinced cooperative members to reduce vine density by half in order to encourage better flavor, which meant sacrificing profits in the short term. He optimistically promised higher prices in return for lower productivity.

To make good on his promises, Dubosc worked national and international angles. He won a new wine appellation, Côtes de Saint-Mont, from the usually slow-moving wine standards board. He built new caves and bottling plants at the cooperative. He traveled the globe to make a name and a market for new Plaimont wines, emphasizing not just high quality for

moderate prices but also worthy old varieties that deserved new life. Always he kept his eye on his own village, his own *terroir:* he helped the local high school start a viticulture program, and supplied interested Plaimont technical consultants as teachers.

The activity on many fronts produced dramatic results. When Dubosc was elected managing director of the cooperative it had 2 employees. Today it has 140.

So far Slow Food has not dared intervene in French wine affairs, perhaps fearing an international diplomatic crisis. But this kind of direct intervention—researching and rescuing rare grape varieties, giving them new life in the international economy—is just what Slow Food tries to do in the Ark. And the efforts to exploit rather than be caught in the web of bureaucracy,

and to find international markets, is what Slow Food does in the Presidia. As Slow Food puts into action its long-planned wide-scale move into France, Dubosc and his success with Plaimont wines can serve as a lodestar.

Dubosc also holds dear the Slow Food idea that eating and drinking are the best methods of persuasion, preferably on-site. He likes to show visitors the wisdom of pairing local grapes with local foods at Auberge de la Bidouze, Plaimont's restaurant of choice and apparently that of every local farmer and businessman as well. Any Bidouze lunch and dinner includes vast portions of foie gras and slices of fattened duck breast and hunks of goose and duck meat cooked and preserved in their own fat—the sort of specialties that every local household still puts up, which were once reserved for special occasions but are now affordable every day. Ducks and geese are raised here on a huge scale, fed on the corn that is the region's chief commodity. A far more frequent sight than vineyards, in fact, are large fields planted with corn.

To check the effects of a cuisine that prides itself on excess, Dubosc orders with barely cooked *(mi-cuit)* slices of duck breast one of Plaimont's newly revived wines of the country—the golden and wonderfully named Pacherenc du Vic Bilh, a full, sweet wine usually sipped as an aperitif or dessert wine. It includes three very local varieties, each with a name nearly as distinctive as the wine's: Petit Courbu, to ensure body and structure; Petit and Gros Manseng, for sweetness; and Arrufiac, with a cleansing acidity at the end. Sauternes and other big, sweet wines, the ones most people would order with foie gras, can stand up to its richness, Dubosc says, as he urges a guest to eat all of what looks like an entire liver that threatens to spill over the sides of a large dinner plate. But those big wines coat the palate with their syrupy power. Pacherenc de Vic Bilh instead defats the tongue and prepares you for the next foray. It's a kind of *trou gascon*—the neat shot of Armagnac tossed back midmeal that gets you ready for cassoulet.

Next, Dubosc demonstrates a more modern pairing: a purply pink slice of ham, cured by his brother, with a rosé that Plaimont recently began marketing as a *vin de soif. Vin de soif*—"wine to slake thirst"—was inspired by the bottles of low-alcohol wine that vineyard workers once kept cool in streams, awaiting their afternoon breaks. In a world where powerful wines are increasing in alcohol to show their muscle and justify their prices, this is a refreshing wine to drink at lunch. Or so Dubosc says: he can make anything sound like a natural idea, and his great charm keeps you from noticing yet another ingenious way to keep alive wine from grapes no one had noticed for decades.

Jancis Robinson, one of the world's most respected writers on wine, and a friend and admirer of Dubosc's, says that this sort of innovation is surprisingly rare. The French stick to what they know, she explains, believing that the rest of the world will follow them, the way it always did. But in the past twenty years, the major rivals and followers of France—America, Australia, Chile, even Canada—have begun following their own paths. Often that means searching out rare grapes that have all but disappeared.

Dubosc knows that Gascony's comparative isolation has been both its obstacle and its blessing. He is one of the few French wine makers who thinks that the way to pioneer a path in the modern world is to return to his home territory's old, slow ways.

"Here, try one of these," Stephen Wood will say to any visitor who follows the sign to Poverty Lane Orchards, a few minutes off a highway that runs through his part of New Hampshire and clear up to Canada. Between two of the weathered barns are big, square slatted bins of apples, stacked nearly as high as the buildings.

The apples don't look anything like what's in a supermarket. They're not big, perfect, and shiny. Rather than chemical-apple green and fire-engine red, they're dusty gold-brown, brushed with deep leaf and topaz. The skins are thick and textured, rather than waxed to a luminous shine. The shapes are different from the familiar high-shouldered Red Delicious or fat-cheeked Granny Smith, but just as beautiful. They're old-fashioned apples—small, wide-waisted, some of them pertly lobed.

Wood picks first a bright, round, healthy red apple, small but nicely filled out. "Esopus Spitzenberg," he says, handing it to a visitor with an introduction that sounds like it's the name of an upstanding New England citizen of the nineteenth century. "They say this was Thomas Jefferson's favorite apple." The flesh is firm and ivory-colored, with a sweet-tart snap and a spicy finish. "You're not just tasting sugar," he says. "That's a very fine dessert apple"—the orchardist's term for fruits intended to be eaten fresh or cooked, rather than pressed into cider. "But it has a high amount of sugar and acidity, too, meaning that it can cross into cider. That made it especially valuable in the nineteenth century, and it's still valuable today."

He reaches into another of the high bins for a thick-skinned, somewhat flattened, topaz-colored apple with hints of red. "Golden Russet," he says. "Famous all over New England and one of the most popular russets"—the name of the brown-tinged apples that remain English favorites. It's easy to love these apples. The flesh is buttery yellow, like Yukon Gold potatoes, delightfully grainy, and just juicy enough to go down easily; the taste is briskly, spicily sweet, something like a Golden Delicious gone wild.

"Now," he says, moving to a less-full bin of smaller apples raked up to one corner, "here's an apple you won't like. I bet you'll have trouble even holding the flesh in your mouth. It's a great cider apple, though." Chistle Jersey is a small,

**FRUIT**
*Stephen Wood*
**NEW HAMPSHIRE**

perfectly round, brownish orange apple with skin like fine sandpaper. The flesh is chewy, mealy, dry, and tannic; tannins produce the dry, astringent quality familiar from unripe bananas. "That's a bittersweet," Wood says. "High in tannins, which stabilize cider and add breadth and complexity. Low in acid, and there's a lot of sugar, too,"

Surprisingly bitter this apple may be, causing a kind of initial involuntary rearing of the head. But Chistle Jersey has such an interesting flavor, with different elements that keep registering on the palate after the initial bite, that you want to keep eating it. After all, good coffee seems impossibly bitter on first tasting.

Apples did not make themselves welcome throughout the colonies because they were pretty to look at or delightful to eat. Crunching into a refreshing, juicy apple had nothing to do with their rapid spread. They were an easy way to produce alcohol in a climate too cold for grapes. Most of the apples that grew in New England were ugly to look at—misshapen, gnarled, with pebbled, russeted skin—and sour and astringent, with a dry, crumbly texture that could make you throw one across the orchard after the first bite.

Those qualities were fine for the cider making the colonists knew from the West Country and in Normandy and Brittany, too. "Cider" in England and in France still means a home brew a bit more alcoholic than beer and a bit less than wine. It meant the same thing in the United States until the Temperance League changed the meaning of cider to fresh apple juice, and created the alcohol-free myth of Johnny Appleseed with which all American children grow up.

The first calamity that befell New England apple growers occurred after World War II. Improved transport, mechanization of orchards, and standardization of supermarkets narrowed the variety of salable apples to just a few, most of them grown in the West. Then, in barely two decades—the 1980s and 1990s—China became a dominant world force in apple growing, with a program to plant millions of acres of the world's best-selling apples and undersell other exporters. South American countries like Brazil, Chile, and Argentina began planting apples, exploiting their own cheap labor. The hemispheric seasonal differences allowed American supermarkets to offer fresh apples year-round. Washington and other states radically improved storage methods, keeping fall apples in ideal condition almost through the spring. But long-term cold storage was expensive, and the mid-sized and big cooperatives that could afford it were growing tasteless varieties already. Even perfectly stored, just-like-fresh apples couldn't compete with apples that were actually fresh.

Wood's father, a country doctor, had a deep love of land. He wanted to protect as much of the rural New Hampshire around him as he could from the developers who were busily building houses and shopping centers around his area of the state—the town of Lebanon, near Dartmouth College. In order to keep buying land, he had to keep up his medical practice. It

was left to Stephen, now married to a college classmate, Louisa Spencer, to think of how the land could be made to pay.

Wood turned first to the varieties that had ready buyers—McIntosh, Cortland, Gala, and Macoun, sweet and fresh-tasting apples with a loyal following throughout New England. They grow well in the rocky New England soil and cold climate. A tall, strapping, handsome man, Wood had started helping out in apple orchards when he was eleven. He loved studying the way apple trees grew, with their tall central branches and outer fruiting ones that can be straggly or dense; he practiced grafting with local orchardists, and knew it would be a lifelong hobby. He had no idea it would become a career.

By the late 1980s, a few years after Wood seriously began growing apples, it became clear that competition had robbed New England growers of the market even for the few apples that were still profitable for them. And China was just starting its massive apple plantings. Wood started experimenting with heirloom dessert apples, reasoning that a smaller amount of high-quality, rare apples with superior flavor could be a more economically productive use of the land.

He planted and built a market among gourmet shops and restaurants for apples like Esopus Spitzenberg, Golden Russet, Wickson, and Pomme Grise, among others. He and Louisa actively encouraged visitors to sample every kind in the small farm stand they outfitted, placing a sharp knife and plate beside half-bushel baskets and describing the attributes and appeal of each apple. Chefs and specialty-store owners loved Poverty Lane Orchards' varieties, and tourists from all over the country and Europe and Asia in search of the flaming fall leaves were enchanted by the beautiful and rarely cultivated apples.

Wood and Spencer knew that sooner or later they would have to try something else. They could transform the farm stand into a

quaint gift shop, but "We didn't want to come home smelling like scented candles every night to persuade ourselves we were running an orchard." They could make applesauce and jams and pies, "adding value" to the crop and hoping that a high retail price could offset the costs of maintaining the apple trees. But they saw what was happening to their fellow growers who went that route. "At some point they have to acknowledge that they could buy fruit to do what they're doing cheaper," Wood says. "The orchard becomes just an aesthetic adjunct."

The value he thought to add was the original American apple value: hard cider. Cider could attract wine buyers, who were used to appreciating and paying for small differences in beverages made from fruit. He visited Bullmers Ciders, the best-known cider producer in England, for an idea of how to choose apples for cider and encourage the best flavor. He grafted dozens of bittersweet and bitter-sharp apples to McIntosh trees.

Then he put his tools to work tuning up the cider presses, which are perhaps the most enchanting part of a picturesque process. The first stage is simple crushing of the apples, which are conveyed up to a hopper and then roughly ground into a pulp, stems, seeds, and all. The mash, which is called pomace and looks something like browned applesauce, is pumped into square bundles that go into slatted metal racks; the racks are then stacked into the press itself. Old-fashioned "rack and cloth" cider presses even have picturesquely named parts: the stack of pomace-filled cloth bundles is called a "cheese." A hydraulically powered screw presses the stack, and the juice tantalizingly drips down the sides into a wide, shallow metal pan.

This is thick, rich, cloudy, amber-colored fresh cider. Its full, spicy flavor may be familiar to New Englanders, but it is unknown to most Americans who are used to the heat-treated, superfiltered apple juice that is misleadingly labeled cider. Unpasteurized cider is also full of wild yeasts, and an indispensable base for fermented cider; the growing American movement of home cider makers prizes but can seldom find it. Some cider makers add sugar to the juice, to increase the alcohol content, which is otherwise much closer to beer than wine. Some add different yeasts, as wine and Champagne makers do, aiming for a house style. Some constantly decant the cider to refine the process, and blend the fermented juices of different apples into barrels to make house blends and house styles.

Wood believes in simplicity. "I want the orchard to be identifiable in the bottle," he says. He mixes the varieties immediately after pressing, adds a simple white wine yeast that will impart no flavor of its own, adds no extra sugar to increase alcohol, and ferments ciders in both steel tanks and oak barrels for flavor. He is also experimenting with single-variety ciders.

His ciders, called Farnum Hill, taste much drier than either fresh or industrially produced alcoholic cider, and have an acidic snap that delights wine lovers. The alcoholic kick is mild, the flavor in the mouth clean.

Fermented ciders have not existed in New England for over a century, and Wood has had to create a market for them. He travels to wine shows and restaurants, freely dispensing tastes. He has also become something of a godfather to other orchard owners and cider makers trying to follow his example—a disconcerting position for someone still experimenting. Farnum Hill ciders, with their complexity and purity of flavor, are showing the way for other New England growers who don't want to abandon their orchards.

Jim Gerritsen leans over a curious tractor, painted garden-pea green, with a few homemade parts sprouting from the base and sides. He takes a small potato and cuts it into four chunks. "One eye apiece," he says. "It's the eyes that sprout." He puts the chunks, some of which have in fact already sprouted, onto a narrow, black rubber conveyor belt at the back of the planter. "This will put each piece into

**VEGETABLES**
*Jim Gerritsen*
**MAINE**

the soil," he says, excitedly moving around the planter to show how it works. "We put this on ourselves," he says, pointing to a spade-shaped length of metal at the front. "Our soil is so rocky it would break an ordinary potato planter."

Gerritsen has rigged this machinery to plant heirloom potatoes in a part of the United States that for more than a century was synonymous with potatoes—the vast Aroostock County of northeastern Maine, which is as big as Connecticut and Rhode Island combined. Aroostock looks little like the Maine that draws tourists from all over the world, the Maine of evergreen-dotted seascapes and lobster boats. It has big sky, wide open plains, and hills covered with pines. It's easy to see why some New Englanders have an almost visceral annual longing to go north, for the hunting, fishing, and incomparably fresh air of Aroostock.

It's easy to see, too, why the farmland appealed to the English and Irish settlers, who recognized that the cool, damp Maine climate would be ideal for potatoes. They also saw that the soil was better than what they had left, even if it was rocky. "Caribou loam," named for the native reindeer that once lived in the Maine woods, has just the right mixture of clay, silt, and sand. Through the 1940s, Maine was the country's largest potato producer, and Aroostock produced 90 percent of Maine potatoes.

Today the Maine woods are being methodically logged by Canadian and American timber companies, and the chief crop of what had been the chief agricultural county in New England has become trees. The acreage devoted to potatoes has shrunk from two hundred thousand in the late 1940s to sixty-three thousand in 2000—a loss of almost 70 percent. The soil is still just as good for potatoes. But the market doesn't want Maine potatoes anymore, which like all potatoes that grow according to nature's temperature and rainfall are uneven in shape.

People now associate Idaho with potatoes, and think of them as long, perfectly even ovals. This is because after McDonald's made potatoes synonymous with fries, in the 1950s, it hijacked the American potato industry. What it wanted was what America grew, and it wanted long, dry, flawlessly shaped potatoes. Once irrigation arrived in the West, growing cycles could be controlled to produce perfectly shaped potatoes— just right for McDonald's.

Jim Gerritsen knew from a young age that he wanted to be a farmer, and he decided that Aroostock County was the best place to do it. His is a particularly unusual story. Gerritsen made his decision in northern California after spending his childhood in San Francisco, a place young people dream of getting to, not leaving.

Farming ran in Gerritsen's blood. Both of his parents had grown up on farms, his father on an apple orchard in Washington and his mother on a cattle and wheat ranch in South Dakota. They were part of the postwar migration from the farm to the city. "My grandfather kept telling my dad that farming was hard, that there wasn't much money in it," Gerritsen says. "My dad listened."

But while studying forestry in a California college, Gerritsen decided that his place was on a farm. To look at him today, that decision seems inevitable: his craggy features, deep-set green eyes, and wind-etched face immediately identify him as a man of the land. The gray-white beard and shoulder-length hair identify him as a child of the idealistic 1960s and the 1970s.

Maine's abandonment of potato farming was what made Gerritsen think he could afford good farmland there. The state was too poor to compete with the lower labor costs and high production of western agricultural states, and also too poor to grow houses instead of potatoes—the fate of most southern New England farms. The demand for perfectly shaped potatoes was recent enough that landowners had not yet had time to plant trees in place of potatoes, so the land was still clear.

Californian child of the '60s that he was, Gerritsen intended to farm organically. The lapse of at least a decade without any kind of crop planting meant that much of the Aroostock farmland would more than meet the requirements of organic farming. He "read every book on the state of Maine" in the Humboldt State College library, and was drawn to Maine's reputation of "good, friendly, down-to-earth people living an outdoor tradition."

The path to potatoes was slow. In 1976, Gerritsen bought the forty-acre Wood Prairie Farm, in the heart of potato-growing territory: a short drive down Route 1 from Presque Isle, a town only a few miles from the Canadian border that is the effective capital of Aroostock County. Farm stands boasting new-crop potatoes, and the offices of potato cooperatives, still line Route 1 between Presque Isle and Bridgewater, where Gerritsen found his farm.

At first he grew what he thought the organic market wanted: various vegetables, apples for cider, pumpkins, and cattle and lambs for organic meat. But none of these paid well enough to support the costs of the farm. Potatoes seemed the least likely savior. What market was left for them

was mostly for "chipping" potatoes—unbeautiful potatoes that would grow in the Maine climate and could still be processed industrially.

A significant portion of the Maine potato market has always been for seed potatoes, which are grown carefully to ensure that they are disease-free. Potatoes left over from the previous year's harvest are likely to be plagued by bacterial, viral, and fungal problems; late blight, which remained a danger to the U.S. crop through the 1980s, caused the Irish potato famines of the 1840s, which killed millions and sent millions of immigrants to the United States. Starting in the 1920s, Maine set itself up as the country's most careful producer of seed potatoes. "Maine certified" meant the safest potatoes; the phrase still carries great weight in the potato world.

The gap Gerritsen could fill was producing certified organic seed potatoes. And the most appealing ones would be heirlooms and other varieties that had long ago fallen out of use.

To find these, and for inspiration on reaching customers directly instead of losing profits to middlemen, Gerritsen listened carefully to Chris Holmes, a Maine farmer who in the early 1980s sold historic potato varieties through a "potato-of-the-month club," which caught on in the emerging gourmet vegetable market. Gerritsen was also helped mightily by his wife, Megan, whom he had met in 1984 through mutual friends. Megan, who had worked on local farms and has family in the central Maine coast, is a good and enthusiastic cook. She helped Gerritsen evaluate the dozens of heirlooms he planted, cooking them in various ways to decide which ones simply "taste good."

The couple decided to go for inner beauty. They had come to the conclusion that anyone who tastes many heirlooms does: yellow-fleshed potatoes generally have a fuller, richer, more buttery flavor, and skin color means little—especially red and purple skins, whose color is usually merely cosmetic. Even the increasingly industrialized organic market grew "faceless, nameless potatoes that yield well and look pretty but don't taste very good," Megan says.

After a few years of planting and sampling over a hundred kinds of potatoes, the couple narrowed to sixteen the potatoes they would grow and ship direct to customers, including a few all-blue and all-red potatoes for novelty. But most of the ones they like have yellow flesh: the familiar Yukon Gold, which has become the most widely available specialty potato with real flavor; Rose Gold, a red-skinned round potato; and Island Sunshine, an exceptionally blight-resistant, creamy-fleshed round potato developed by two passionate Dutch-born organic breeders on nearby Prince Edward Island, another longtime potato-growing capital.

Fingerlings, popular for their long, thin shape (for which they are named) and their often superior flavor, are prominent in the Wood Prairie catalog: Russian Banana and Swedish Peanut, both of them among the best-tasting fingerlings and both yellow-fleshed, and the Gerritsens' favorite, Rose Finn Apple, a rare yellow-fleshed fingerling with pink skin. The couple honors state tradition by growing round white potatoes, the kind that brought Maine fame and that fell out of favor. Instead of Green Mountain and Irish Cobbler, the traditional varieties, they find old-fashioned round potatoes with better flavor, like Onaway and one developed at Cornell University called Prince Hairy.

Wood Prairie potatoes arrive in neat paper bags with a few holes punched in them for air. The back of the bag is illustrated with a drawing of the Gerritsen family, which has grown to include three young children. The potatoes inside still have a dusting of dirt. They have only been brushed before packing: washing, the standard industry preparation, leaves potatoes vulnerable to rot. Stitched to each bag is a handsome postcard with a drawing modeled on the colorful fruit-crate labels that served as art in early-twentieth-century America.

Selling by catalog keeps the family in touch with potato eaters all over the country. Customers send contented reports and recipe tips to the couple at their Web site. Most of the tips are for potatoes, naturally, but many are for bread. Why bread? Growers must rotate their crops, to avoid depleting soil of the nitrogen and other nutrients that potatoes, a hungry nightshade, need. The Gerritsens plant potatoes only every four years in a given field, and so in any year just ten of their forty acres are planted in potatoes. In the off years, they follow traditional Maine practice and plant spring wheat and oats, to act as nurse crops for clover. Rather than sell off the rotation crops, Megan created a line of organic whole-grain bread mixes—and a bread-mix-of-the-month club to sell it.

Among the customers the Gerritsens treasure most are the gardeners who have come to rely on the trustworthiness of Wood Prairie Farm's certified organic seed potatoes. Advising gardeners on techniques that have worked for them, and describing which varieties might work best in their soil, keeps the couple in touch with people all over the country, and also gives them a hint of warmth in the long, long Maine winter.

But the contact the Gerritsens prize most is with their own community. The people they hire are strictly local, many of them teenagers who know the region's potato heritage but have never had the chance to participate in it. Megan tells of one of the best helpers at Wood Prairie Farm, a young man named Luke Bradstreet, who began working with them when he was thirteen. He has put his welding studies at a local technical college to good use, helping Jim custom-build his farm equipment. It was Luke who put the rock-shooing spade on the potato planter Jim is so proud of. Like most young graduates, Luke plans to go to southern Maine—the part of the state that lives on summer tourism and rich summer people, where decent-paying jobs are easier to find. But those jobs don't help the land, and love of the land is what drew the Gerritsens here.

"He'll be back," Megan says. "He'll stay away till he realizes he's an Aroostock guy."

Most people worry about the destruction of the world's rain forests. Some people do something about it. One couple is on an admittedly eccentric quest to rescue the most useful plants of rain forests all over the world and keep them safe in a reserve protected from political turmoil, industrial polluters, and rapacious oil drillers. Working with no government or foundation funding, no inde-

**BOTANICAL ARK**
*Alan and Susan Carle*
**AUSTRALIA**

pendent means, and few able bodies other than their own, the couple combs rain forests in countries as far-flung as New Guinea, Malaysia, Cameroon, Mauritius, Borneo, Madagascar, Colombia, Ecuador, and Brazil, looking for endangered plants that could someday save the world. Guided by local shamans and healers and in the face of often fearsome local obstacles— including corrupt and sometimes violent policemen, not to mention tempests and floods—they discover plants just as they are coming into flower, and carefully collect and clean the seeds. Then they spirit the seeds home and plant them. Trees shoot up in a year or two. Fruits and flowers appear in months. Most everything that grows is edible. This magic garden is called the Botanical Ark, and it's a world away.

Alan and Susan Carle could spring from the sort of fairy tale their garden evokes. Their first replanting was of themselves: he from upper New York state, she from Brooklyn, both as teenagers, both to a country where they knew no one. Alan Carle, a robust man in his early fifties, says that he knew he "belonged" in Australia

from the time when, as a young adolescent, he read an article on the South Pacific in *National Geographic*. Even though he had never traveled farther than Florida and hardly had a dime, he bought a one-way ticket to Australia when he was nineteen. Carle knew he loved water, and thought he might study marine biology. His real aim was to make good on what he had for years said he wanted to be when he grew up: Australian.

Once he had enrolled himself at a university in Queensland, the northeastern Australia state across from the Great Barrier Reef, Alan sent for Susan to come help him with field research. He had met the classically pretty girl at an Adirondacks summer camp. He was fifteen, and she was just ten, sent to the camp by the Norwegian Children's Home in Brooklyn, where she was raised. After a year at Brooklyn College, she decided to go on a six-month break and take Alan up on his invitation. A young woman who had never lived outside a city and had never even been allowed into a kitchen soon found herself living in a hut in the rain forest without electricity or running water and collecting wood every night for the cookstove. Six months turned into twenty-five years.

The Queensland rain forest is the world's oldest, and the climate is ideal for growing anything that flourishes in the jungle. Yet European farmers cleared the natural vegetation to raise sugarcane, to graze cattle for beef, and to plant European fruits for which there was a market, like apples and pears. They fought the climate.

Alan reasoned that farmers should instead look to create a market for fruits, flowers, and nuts that grow easily in rain forests. He read about dozens of rain forest fruits that had been in commercial production until a few decades before. As with industrial food production everywhere, flavor was a priority that fell far

behind productivity, hardiness, and suitability for shipping. Secondary species fell out of cultivation and even out of consciousness. The forests were vanishing even faster.

The couple, by then married and starting a family, found an ideal site for their dream farm: thirty acres of abandoned cattle farmland an hour above Cairns, the capital of Queensland, surrounded by the protected Daintree National Park, a lush rain forest declared a World Heritage Site. The original idea was to build a full-service ark in three five-year stages. First, identify the most important plants not yet in the country and seek them out, with a priority on putting in the plants that took the longest to grow. Second, do the same with animals. Third, plant and create new sources of alternative energy.

Fruits and nuts proved to be of consuming fascination. Nearly twenty years later, Alan says, "We're still on the first five-year plan."

To pay for the land and collecting expeditions, Alan worked as a builder and gardener and Susan as a waitress and teacher. The two alternated shifts to allow one to work away from home and the other to work in the garden and stay with their two daughters. Growing fruits on a scale large enough to make money proved too time-consuming, but flowers did provide a way to make the land pay for itself. For a few years, the Carles were Australia's largest grower of tropical flowers, selling species they brought back from collecting trips and opening a new market in a country whose florists bought little beyond roses and carnations.

Their lives and their expeditions were fueled by credit cards and anxiety. Nonetheless, looking for help from any government or institution was out of the question from the start. This adamant refusal stems from Alan's stubborn independence. More important, Alan says, he would never want to betray the tribal elders, local plant enthusiasts, and botanists who have led him to secret places and given him secret plants. The understanding is that no one will ever profit from the plants except the people living where they grow. Nor will the Carles ever endanger a plant's survival in its native habitat. "Taking a couple of seeds out of their environment won't do any damage," Alan says. "It's when you destroy the environment that you cause problems."

Today the Carles support the Ark primarily by inviting groups of visitors and giving them a walk in the garden and a meal cooked from the garden harvests. The ride from Cairns, an appealingly loose tourist city full of backpackers on their way to or from the Barrier Reef or the Daintree park, passes dramatic beachsides and the road into the village of Port Douglas, a kind of latter-day Portofino for movie stars in search of tropical paradise.

It seems impossible that twenty years ago this land was bare. The drive to the house winds through bamboo forests, groves of philodendrons of science-fiction hugeness, kapok trees with trunks of vast girth, and palms higher than telephone poles. A walk through the garden, as the Carles call it, is really a walk around the Equator: they have re-created the world's principal tropical zones in miniature as a way of demonstrating the amazing range of uses a rain forest can offer if it is left alone to grow. "Now we're going into Africa," Susan will say as a visitor goes down a path lined with trees and shrubs native to various African countries. While there, visitors must eat a berry from the miracle fruit tree, or dulcificum, native to Nigeria. The bright red berry, which looks like a yew berry but isn't poisonous, has the curious effect of rendering everything you eat for the next hour or so saccharine-sweet. Susan or Alan pass out fresh lemon slices to prove the miracle, which is caused by a protein in the berry that blocks acid receptors on the tongue.

The Carles conclude their walks with a meal featuring herbs and fruits picked that morning, often including one of Susan's superb Thai curries with fresh turmeric, curry leaves, galangal, red pepper, lemongrass, kaffir lime leaf, and any of a hundred gingers the couple grows. Susan places all the ingredients on a tray for visitors to examine, just as she dug or cut them. A salad follows, sprinkled with cloche-shaped costus flowers in pale yellow, pink, and white.

But the real centerpiece is a selection of sliced fruits. The choice is seldom a problem: at any time of the year, at least thirty fruits are available, and in summer months as many as eighty. Susan combines familiar fruits with unfamiliar variations: blue Thai bananas with a citrus tartness; yellow "lemon" papayas with a hint of lemon and flesh so pale it seems albino; yellow and pink-purple passionfruit—fruits startlingly new to most visitors.

After a meal, the Carles recount a few of their adventures, giving an idea of what it takes to keep the Ark going. Customs officials in Africa have brandished guns at the border, demanding bribes for the safe passage of seeds and plants. The opposition they encounter does not end when they get home. Australian customs officials may not be armed, but their requirements are stringent and becoming ever more so. To protect their lovingly gathered seeds from damage at the hands of customs inspectors, the Carles built their own quarantine house at the Ark— a small greenhouse with double doors and an airlock, extremely fine-meshed window screens, and special drainage so that no pest or disease can escape into the environment. They pay inspectors to come and check their seeds.

Everything is worth it for the joy they take in the day-to-day work, however frenetic it may be, and in the joy of discovery. Alan describes a long search for an exceedingly rare fruit, about which he had e-mailed a friend and collaborator in Ecuador. In ten years of looking, the friend had never been able to find a ripe fruit. Last year on a trip there, Alan says, "I headed off on the last afternoon, and got in a magical forest. Within a couple of hours, I found what I'm sure was the only ripe fruit in the forest. Somebody's on my side."

THE RECIPES

**SLOW FOOD IS ANYTHING THAT USES INGRE-**
dients carefully raised and tended and that tastes of where it's from. Most important, it bears the stamp of the hands and the kitchen that made it. Here's how to imprint that taste on your own dishes with the help of a wide-ranging collection of recipes from cooks in Europe and America who share Slow Food's celebration of the good, the simple, the handmade.

The order of the cooks is Old World to New, starting in Italy, birthplace of Slow Food, and skipping across western Europe and over the ocean to America. The last stop is the San Francisco Bay Area, which makes a kind of full circle. With its almost fanatical attention to where and how food was raised, the Bay Area resembles no place as much as Italy.

The thread that unites these many cooks and the many cultures drawn from is a love of ingredients as they grow and then are transformed into dishes. All these cooks love finding food, knowing the people who grew it, and contentedly working with it to share meals, however primitive or bountiful, with friends.

"HE'S THE MOST CHARISMATIC KID I'VE EVER met," Susie Cushner, the photographer for this book, said after spending a day with Fulvio Marino. Fulvio is one of three generations of six Marino men whose name start with *F*. The grandfather, Felice, knows every brook and practically every tree in the hills around Cossano Belbo, a town in the truffle-and-Barolo-rich region of Piedmont, very near Bra, the home of Slow Food. The landscape was his friend and protector in his days as a partisan fighting fascists and Nazis in World War II.

Fulvio and all the *F* men grow and mill "eight-row" corn, an older, lower-yielding variety that makes more flavorful polenta. They also mill old varieties of wheat between stones that they incise and sharpen by hand. The family takes part in numerous organic-food organizations and brings its cheerful demeanor, not to mention its wonderful polenta, to food shows across the country.

The irrepressible Fulvio explains to visitors how the family gives farmers seed corn to make sure the corn grows true, and why the old variety tastes so much better even though it's hard to grow. He himself helps deliver seed corn to local farmers, and takes a

lively interest in the welfare of the families who live in the plains and hills. Like his grandfather, he seems to want to know every house, every family around the Marino mill.

Fulvio's favorite activity is showing visitors his home paths, the secret hilltop refuges where he, his brother Fausto, and their friends hatch schemes for their future. That future includes an intimate connection with the past.

# POLENTA WITH BAGNA DL'INFERN

*Visitors lucky enough to be invited to the Marino family's kitchen will have the pleasure of polenta made several ways. If they offer to help with the dishes, they can sneak some of the special treat of crisp polenta that sticks to the sides and bottom of the pot.* ❋ *The family's favorite sauce is* bagna dl'infern, *the devil's own sauce, named for the cayenne pepper the usually benign female cooks add to make it lightly spicy. It's an anchovy sauce, anchovies being a great Piedmont specialty, made with garlic and olive oil. The same trinity of ingredients is used for the Piedmont's famed warm dipping sauce,* bagna cauda. *But this is mellowed by a tomato-sauce base. The family usually passes bowls of chopped hard-boiled egg and tuna as garnishes for those who want to make a full meal of the dressed polenta. It's especially wonderful with oil-packed Sicilian tuna.*

❋ ❋ ❋ ❋ ❋ ❋ ❋ ❋ ❋

**SAUCE:**
6 tablespoons extra-virgin
    olive oil
1 onion, finely diced
1 carrot, finely diced

1 stalk celery, finely diced
Cayenne pepper to taste
6 cloves garlic, minced
8 salt-packed anchovies, rinsed
    and coarsely chopped
1½ cups tomato sauce

**POLENTA:**
8 cups water
1 tablespoon salt, plus more to
    taste if needed
2 cups polenta

❋ ❋ ❋ ❋ ❋ ❋ ❋ ❋ ❋

**TO MAKE THE SAUCE:** Heat 3 tablespoons of the olive oil in a medium sauté pan or skillet over medium heat and add the onion, carrot, celery, and cayenne. Sauté until the onion is translucent, about 3 minutes. Add the garlic and anchovies and cook, stirring frequently, until the anchovies begin to melt and the garlic is fragrant, 2 to 3 minutes. Add the tomato sauce, reduce the heat, and gently simmer the sauce for 10 minutes. Stir in the remaining 3 tablespoons olive oil.

**TO MAKE THE POLENTA:** In a medium, heavy pot, bring the water to a boil. Add the

1 tablespoon salt and gradually whisk in the polenta. Continue to whisk until the polenta starts to thicken. Reduce the heat to low, switch to a wooden spoon, and continue to simmer for 30 to 40 minutes, stirring frequently so that the polenta doesn't stick to the bottom and burn. If the polenta becomes too thick, add a ladle or two of water. Taste and adjust the seasoning, if necessary.

To serve, ladle the polenta into warmed, shallow bowls and pour some of the sauce on top.

**SERVES 8 AS A FIRST COURSE**

GIUSEPPE GARIBALDI SPENT MANY YEARS AS A STE-
vedore on the Genoa docks before being able to make his
family farm, in the steep hills of Liguria, thrive again. With
his savings, he convinced his mother, Maria Ines, to cook at a tiny, lovely restaurant and
inn, Cà di Gòsita, that he opened in the farmhouse. The family specialty is cooking "under
the *campana,*" or terra-cotta cloche, on the floor of a wood-fired oven.

Diners feel like guests in a farm family, because that's what they are. Fellow guests
usually include local politicians and professionals who make their way up the hill for a taste
of local history they simply can't get elsewhere anymore. Not every mother has the same
knowledge of local food in her hands that Maria Ines does, nor a son willing to build a
little house off the terrace just for the huge hearth.

The most spectacular, and most Ligurian, thing that mother and son cook are
*testaroli,* thick crepes cooked in molds, painted with pesto, and piled up like a stack of flap-
jacks. The molds, with medieval checkered patterns, are emblematic of this part of Liguria.
So, of course, is pesto, made with the tiny-leaved basil that grows in plastic-coated green-
houses up and down the surrounding hillsides.

# PESTO ALLA GENOVESE

*This pesto is good on almost anything—certainly crepes, potatoes quartered and boiled (an especially popular combination in Liguria), and maybe even pancakes low on sugar. If you've never made pesto by hand, please try this recipe. Not only will you experience the reanimating "exhilaration" the writer Patience Gray says comes from pounding fresh, fragrant things, but you'll also have an incomparably creamy pesto to put on pasta for a simple, yet full, supper.*

2 large cloves garlic
Kosher salt to taste
2 bunches Genoese (small-leaved) basil, about 36 leaves per bunch, or any available small-leaved green basil
7 tablespoons pine nuts, lightly toasted
¼ cup grated pecorino cheese, preferably Sardinian
¼ cup grated Parmigiano-Reggiano cheese
6 tablespoons olive oil, preferably Ligurian extra-virgin, plus more as needed

In a medium stone mortar, pound the garlic and pinch of salt into a smooth paste with a pestle. Gradually add the basil leaves, continuing to pound. Add the pine nuts and both cheeses and pound into a smooth paste. Add the 6 tablespoons olive oil, drop by drop, grinding the pestle in a circular motion until the pesto is completely amalgamated. Add more olive oil to adjust the taste or texture as you like. Season with salt.

**MAKES 1 CUP, ENOUGH FOR 1 POUND OF PASTA**

**NOTE:** Add 1 or 2 teaspoons of pasta water to the pesto to make it creamy before tossing with pasta or potatoes.

ELENA ROVERA PERSONIFIES THE HIGHEST AIM OF Slow Food, and even though she is far from an official part of it—she believes in acting only locally—she's a few minutes down the road from its headquarters, in the lush, hilly farmland of Piedmont. There she gathers together young people educated by their hardworking parents for something "better" than farming and rallies them to take a step back in time, to organic methods of raising fruits and vegetables long out of use.

Elena Rovera's husband, Raffaele, was the inspiration for her crusade. For too many years, she watched in the late fall as he was forced to sell at a loss the heirloom pears and apples he raised on his father's and grandfather's farm. The prices were dictated by wholesalers who could buy rival fruit from big industrial farms and eastern European countries with minimal prices for labor. Elena wanted to try selling their products direct to the customer, and perhaps that way be able to realize a profit.

Thus was born the rural cooperative that provides the couple with daily financial headaches and daily inspiration for the soul. It has expanded to include dozens of members, mostly small farms trying to grow heirloom fruits and vegetables using organic or environmentally friendly farming techniques. Each member has a different and fascinating story, a story Elena learns and tells other members before asking them to vote in a new farmer or artisan.

Tourists on the Piedmont truffle trail can taste all the products of the farm at Cascina del Cornale, a small restaurant on the main road between Alba and Asti, where Rovera has a farmers' market and serves the kind of simple, rustic food most visitors hope to find but seldom do. They can also buy the organic produce, cheeses, and preserves of the member farms.

# CHICKEN CACCIATORE WITH BAKED POTATOES

*Here is comfort food with a great sauce for sopping, made even better by a Piedmont red wine both in the stewpot and the diner's glass. Any heirloom potato will be at its best this way; the widely available Yukon Gold will do nicely, too.*

❋ ❋ ❋ ❋ ❋ ❋ ❋ ❋ ❋

1 chicken, about 3¾ pounds
Salt and freshly ground black
    pepper to taste
3 tablespoons olive oil
1 red onion, cut into
    ¼-inch dice

1 carrot, peeled and cut into
    ¼-inch dice
2 stalks celery, cut into
    ¼-inch dice
2 cloves garlic, minced
Leaves from one 1-inch rosemary
    sprig, coarsely chopped

1 cup Roero Arneis wine, or
    any Cabernet
1 cup tomato sauce
1 cup water
Baked Potatoes (recipe follows)

❋ ❋ ❋ ❋ ❋ ❋ ❋ ❋ ❋

Rinse and pat the chicken dry. Cut the chicken into 8 serving pieces and season with a generous amount of salt and black pepper. Heat a large sauté pan or skillet over medium-high heat and add the olive oil. Add the chicken and cook until golden brown on both sides, about 15 minutes total. Transfer the chicken to a platter and set aside.

Add the onion, carrot, celery, garlic, rosemary, and a pinch of salt to the pan. Cook over medium-high heat until the onion is translucent, about 3 minutes. Add the wine and stir to scrape up the browned bits from the bottom of the pan. Cook for 8 to 10 minutes to burn off the alcohol and slightly reduce the wine. Return the chicken to the pan, along with any juices on the platter. Add the tomato sauce and water. Turn the chicken once or twice to mix the ingredients and coat the chicken. Cover the pan, reduce the heat to low, and cook until tender, about 25 to 30 minutes. To serve, place the chicken on a warmed platter with the potatoes on the side.

**SERVES 4 AS A MAIN COURSE**

# BAKED POTATOES

2 ¼ pounds Yukon Gold potatoes the size of a fist, peeled and cut into thick wedges

¼ cup extra-virgin olive oil

1 clove garlic, minced

Leaves from one 2-inch rosemary sprig, coarsely chopped

Salt and freshly ground black pepper to taste

✳ ✳ ✳ ✳ ✳ ✳ ✳ ✳ ✳

Preheat the oven to 350°F. Cook the potatoes in salted simmering water until they can be easily pierced with a knife but still hold their shape, 8 to 10 minutes. Using a slotted spoon, transfer to a baking dish.

In a small bowl, combine the olive oil, garlic, and rosemary. Drizzle the oil mixture over the potatoes and gently toss them with your hands to coat them evenly. Sprinkle with salt and pepper. Cover the dish with aluminum foil and bake the potatoes in the oven until fragrant and heated through, about 15 minutes.

**SERVES 4 AS A SIDE DISH**

# RISOTTO WRAPPED IN CABBAGE LEAVES

*The valley of the Po River, which runs clear across northern Italy, still grows the short-grain rice that gave today's gastronomic world risotto but for centuries gave the region a subsistence grain and a subsistence living. This recipe yields the kind of family dinner that would make a bit of meat go a long way. It's subtle and quiet in flavor, like so much true Italian food, letting you enjoy the soft fullness of the fully cooked rice and cabbage.*

❋ ❋ ❋ ❋ ❋ ❋ ❋ ❋ ❋

16 cabbage leaves
½ cup Arborio rice
Salt to taste

2 tablespoons, plus ¼ cup
    extra-virgin olive oil,
    preferably Ligurian
5 ounces ground veal
2 eggs

5 tablespoons grated
    Parmigiano-Reggiano cheese
Freshly ground black pepper
    to taste
Flour for dredging

❋ ❋ ❋ ❋ ❋ ❋ ❋ ❋ ❋

In a large pot of salted boiling water, cook the cabbage until tender, 2 to 3 minutes. Drain and set aside.

Bring a medium saucepan of water to a boil over high heat. Add the rice and a generous pinch of salt and cook until the rice is tender, about 20 minutes. Drain and set aside.

Heat the 2 tablespoons olive oil in a sauté pan or skillet over high heat. Add the veal, season with a pinch of salt, and cook until the meat browns, about 5 minutes. In a medium bowl, combine the veal, rice, eggs, cheese, a pinch of salt, and a generous amount of black pepper. Stir thoroughly until it forms a smooth mixture.

Pat the cabbage leaves dry and lay them out flat on a work surface. Trim away the tough mid-rib at the base of each leaf, if necessary. Put 1 tablespoon of the veal mixture in the center of each leaf. Fold the sides of the leaves toward the center and roll up from the bottom.

Lightly dredge each cabbage roll in flour. Heat the ¼ cup olive oil in a large sauté pan or skillet over medium-high heat. Add the cabbage rolls and fry on both sides until golden brown. Serve hot.

**SERVES 6 TO 8 AS A FIRST COURSE**

Elena Rovera

# MADERNASSA PEARS WITH BIRBET WINE

*Nearly every visitor to Cascina del Cornale tastes these wine-rich, concentrated baked pears at dessert. It's a simple recipe that will show off any firm-fleshed pear, such as Bosc, to advantage, but is even better with lightly spicy pears like Seckel—or, of course, the small, pretty, plump Madernassas that are the Rovera family heritage and inspiration for its ambitious cooperative.*

❋ ❋ ❋ ❋ ❋ ❋ ❋ ❋ ❋

8 firm Madernassa, Seckel, or Bosc pears

1½ cups moderately sweet red wine

¾ cup Barbera wine or other dry, full-bodied red wine

¼ cup plus 2 tablespoons sugar

1 stick cinnamon

3 whole cloves

❋ ❋ ❋ ❋ ❋ ❋ ❋ ❋ ❋

Preheat the oven to 325°F. Trim the bottom of the pears so that they can stand upright. Put the pears in a baking dish, flat-side down. Add the wines, sugar, cinnamon, and cloves. Bake, basting often, until the pears can be easily pierced with a knife, about 1 hour.

Serve warm or at room temperature, with the spiced wine.

**SERVES 4**

LOTHAR TUBBESING WAS ONE OF THE FIRST SLOW Food converts outside Italy, and helped galvanize countrymen in his northern German city of Lübeck, on the Baltic Sea, to rally round the cause. Until Slow Food USA took hold, Germany had more Slow Food members than any other country outside Italy, thanks partly to Tubbesing's generous work and help.

Tubbesing and his wife, Heike, run one of the most romantic restaurants in a romantic city, famous as the home of Thomas Mann and marzipan—and also as a home of herring, the salting of which made Lübeck a mighty medieval power and the richest of the Baltic cities in the Hanseatic League, a trading union that endured into the twentieth century.

The beautiful Restaurant Lachswehr occupies a mansion built in the Renaissance château style favored in the nineteenth century, on a site that has been occupied by an inn or a restaurant since 1188. The very tall, lean Tubbesing takes great pride in Lachswehr's history, and in Lübeck's. Two of Germany's sprightliest odes to May were written in the garden behind the mansion—one of them set to music by Mozart, Tubbesing will tell guests, as often as not breaking into song. When he shows visitors around the beautifully preserved town center, he seems more like the mayor than a restaurateur.

At the restaurant, the Tubbesings prepare many traditional dishes, often with a modern and sometimes Italian flair. May, the month that inspired that famous ode, brings locally grown fat, white asparagus—another glory of German spring—piled in wide stacks on every surface of the kitchen. All seasons bring salted fish and potatoes, staples of German cooking and keystones of local economic and agricultural history. Rather than slavish adherence to traditional cuisine, the couple's aim is to honor it and bring it forward by using only local ingredients.

# GRAVLAX WITH CITRUS

*Salmon gave Restaurant Lachswehr its very name (Lachs is "salmon" in German); noblemen granted citizens the right to catch salmon on the site. To honor the history, the Tubbesings always offer home-cured gravlax, which they give a welcome citrus zing. Like all gravlax, this recipe is fun to make. It's also sweeter than most, both to balance the citrus and nod to the German love of sweet and sour.*

❄ ❄ ❄ ❄ ❄ ❄ ❄ ❄ ❄

One 1-pound king salmon fillet,
    skin on, pin bones removed
⅓ cup salt

⅔ cup sugar
4 tablespoons grated carrot
4 thin slices lemon

4 thin slices lime
4 thin slices orange
Leaves from a few dill sprigs

❄ ❄ ❄ ❄ ❄ ❄ ❄ ❄ ❄

Cut the salmon fillet in half horizontally. Put the skin half in a glass or stainless-steel dish, skin-side down.

Combine the salt and sugar in a small bowl. Sprinkle half of the mixture evenly over the fish. Distribute 2 tablespoons of the grated carrot over the salt mixture. Place 2 slices of each type of citrus and half of the dill on top. The surface of the fish should be evenly covered with the ingredients.

Place the second half of salmon on top as if you were making a sandwich and layer the remaining ingredients on top in the same order. Wrap the salmon tightly in cheesecloth, return it to the dish, cover, and refrigerate for 36 hours.

Scrape off the citrus, herbs, and any undissolved salt mixture. Serve immediately, or store in the refrigerator for up to 1 week. To serve, cut the salmon into very thin diagonal slices.

**SERVES 4 TO 6 AS A FIRST COURSE**

# PICKLED HERRING WITH APPLES AND CRÈME FRAÎCHE

*Most any hausfrau will greet guests with herring in a creamy apple-and-onion sauce. It takes just minutes to prepare, as the sauce for pickled herring is always on hand in the refrigerator. Any herring from a supermarket jar, rinsed first and put into this sauce, will be improved. To understand the greatness of a dish beloved in its homeland but little appreciated here, order herring by mail from the best U.S. purveyor, Russ & Daughters (800-787-7229). And if you want to cut down on the butterfat content—a most un-German desire—substitute yogurt for the crème fraîche.*

❊ ❊ ❊ ❊ ❊ ❊ ❊ ❊

1½ cups crème fraîche
¾ cup mayonnaise
1 onion, cut into ⅛-inch dice
2 apples, peeled, cored, and cut
    into ⅛-inch dice

2 pickled gherkins or
    cornichons, cut into
    ⅛-inch dice
Salt, freshly ground white
    pepper, and sugar to taste

1½ pounds pickled herring
    fillets, cut into 2-inch
    chunks

❊ ❊ ❊ ❊ ❊ ❊ ❊ ❊

In a small bowl, combine the crème fraîche, mayonnaise, onion, apples, gherkins or cornichons, and a pinch of salt, white pepper, and sugar. Stir to combine.

Put the herring in a medium bowl and gently toss with the sauce. Taste and adjust the seasoning, if necessary. Cover and refrigerate for at least 3 hours before serving. This is best when served the same day.

**SERVES 4 TO 6 AS A FIRST COURSE**

# RÖTE GRÜTZE

*This is the classic German dessert, a sort of thickened clear berry soup served cold, usually with big dollops of whipped cream, sour cream, or crème fraîche. It is as ingrained in the national psyche as summer pudding (page 152) is in Britain. Each tradition shows off the abundance of lovely berries that grow in northern climes—and grow right outside Restaurant Lachswehr's door, where city-leased gardens run alongside canals for miles. The city leases the generous-sized plots for a modest sum to local citizens, who build inventive cabin refuges and enjoy endless summer evenings in the beautiful and bountiful gardens they create.*

✳ ✳ ✳ ✳ ✳ ✳ ✳ ✳ ✳

2¼ pounds fresh or frozen berries, such as strawberries, raspberries, red currants, or black currants

½ cup cornstarch
About 2 tablespoons water
2 cups sugar, plus more for sprinkling

✳ ✳ ✳ ✳ ✳ ✳ ✳ ✳ ✳

If using fresh strawberries, hull and quarter them. Put the cornstarch in a small bowl and whisk in just enough water to dissolve any lumps. Set aside.

In a medium, heavy pot, combine the berries and the 2 cups sugar. Stir to mix. Stirring constantly, bring the berries to a simmer over medium heat, then immediately stir in the cornstarch. Let the mixture return to a simmer, then remove the pot from the heat. Pour into glass bowls and sprinkle the surface with sugar to prevent a skin from forming. Refrigerate until ready to serve.

**SERVES 8 TO 10**

GEORGETTE DUBOS IS THE SPIRITED AND GENEROUS hostess of Auberge de la Bidouze, her inn and restaurant near the village of Saint-Mont in southwest France. She has a large tradition to live up to: every farm in the Gers, as her part of the Southwest is called, raises a few ducks to fatten, and every family puts up its own confit and foie gras. Practically every farm family makes its own wine or gets it from a relative. To compete with the lively tradition of homemade cuisine, she must set a good table.

The daily crowd at her pleasant, big restaurant proves that she does. It's a sort of cafeteria for local businessmen, but these local businessmen know their *plats* and *vins*. They are the farmers who grow on an industrial scale the corn that feeds the flocks of ducks and geese, and the wine makers who traditionally make red wines that the big Armagnac houses blend into their high-priced, internationally known brandy.

Dubos and André Brule, the big, hearty chef, serve a slightly dressed-up version of local cuisine. Among their most devoted patrons is André Dubosc, the fervent admirer of the region who has helped bring it renown with his innovative work at the local Plaimont wine cooperative (see pages 61–64). When Dubos sees Dubosc (no relation; many local names sound alike) come in with an international visitor at lunch, she'll immediately uncork a wine for a welcoming aperitif. The wine won't be Plaimont. That would be too obvious, and deprive the hostess of her right to Southwestern sass. With one of her giant-sized plates of fresh foie gras, though, she'll relent, and make sure the visitor gets a full taste of Gers— both its spirit and its cuisine.

# GARBURE

*Georgette Dubos recommends that every guest start with this deeply flavored soup—a hallmark of Southwest France, where there is a duck in every pot, and also confit and ham. The ham is either made at home or bought from nearby Bayonne, the port that became legendary for* jambon *because of its centrality, supply of local salt, and strong sea breezes.* ✳ *A ham bone will bring vital depth to these winter vegetables, but so will any meaty bone, and the meat can be shredded and put back into the soup. The ideal flavoring is confit, which you can usually find either jarred or canned at gourmet shops—likely produced down the road from Bidouze.* ✳ *This soup is flexible, forgiving, and brothy. It can stay on the stove or in the fridge for days, and is also the basis of the traditional farmer's breakfast:* chabrot, *leftover soup mixed with a healthy shot of Armagnac and sipped from a* calotte, *shaped like a mustache cup.*

✳ ✳ ✳ ✳ ✳ ✳ ✳ ✳

1½ cups dried white filet beans, such as cannellini or haricots tarbais, soaked overnight
5 cloves garlic
1 bay leaf
¾ teaspoon salt, plus more to taste

3 slices smoked bacon, cut into ¼-inch crosswise pieces
1 jambon de Bayonne ham bone or prosciutto ham bone
4 quarts water
2 stalks celery, cut into ½-inch dice
½ head green cabbage, cored and cut into ½-inch pieces

2 potatoes, peeled and cut into ½-inch dice
6 ounces turnips, cut into ½-inch dice (about 1½ cups)
2 legs or thighs from confit of duck
Freshly ground black pepper to taste

✳ ✳ ✳ ✳ ✳ ✳ ✳ ✳

Drain the beans and put them in a medium saucepan. Cover with water by 1 inch and add 1 of the garlic cloves, the bay leaf, and the ¾ teaspoon salt. Bring to a boil and reduce the heat to a simmer. Simmer gently until the beans are tender, about 1 to 2 hours. Remove from heat and let cool in the broth.

Heat a soup pot over medium heat and add the bacon. Fry the bacon until crisp and golden brown. Using a slotted spoon, transfer to paper towels to drain. Pour off the fat from the pot.

To the same pot, add the ham or prosciutto bone and water. Bring to a boil, reduce the heat to a simmer, and skim the surface if necessary. Add the remaining 4 cloves garlic, the celery, bacon, and a generous pinch of salt. Simmer

gently for about 10 minutes. Add the cabbage, potatoes, and turnips. Return the soup to a simmer and cook for another 10 minutes. Drain the beans and add them to the pot. Taste and adjust the seasoning, if necessary. Simmer the soup until all of the ingredients are tender, 10 to 15 minutes.

Meanwhile, remove and discard the skin from the duck confit. Pull the meat from the bone and shred it into small chunks. When all of the vegetables are cooked, stir the confit meat into the pot and remove it from the heat.

Ladle the soup into warmed soup bowls. Finish each bowl with a few twists of black pepper.

**SERVES 10 AS A MAIN COURSE**

# PANFRIED DUCK BREAST WITH SWEET SAUCE

*This is the simplest and best way to enjoy duck breast, which at Bidouze is served in plate-covering slices. But even nonfattened duck is very rich, and this surprisingly easy sauce makes up for any richness lost in the translation. It would turn any sautéed or roasted poultry into an occasion. ❋ The local fortified wine is red, deep, and sweet. Try a cream sherry or, even better, Madeira, if you can't find the true taste of Gascony.*

| | | |
|---|---|---|
| ¼ cup sugar | 1 tablespoon duck fat | ⅔ cup crème fraîche |
| 2 tablespoons water | ¼ cup Floc de Gascogne, | 4 duck breast halves |
| 1¼ cups chicken stock | Madeira, or cream sherry | |

In a small, heavy saucepan, combine the sugar and water. Cover and bring to a boil over medium-high heat. Uncover and cook until the sugar begins to caramelize. Reduce the heat to medium-low and carefully add the chicken stock, duck fat, and wine. Gently simmer the sauce for 1 hour.

Whisk in the crème fraîche. Continue to whisk and simmer until the sauce thickens, about 10 minutes. Set aside and keep warm.

With a sharp knife, carefully score the skin of each duck breast in a diagonal crisscross pattern without piercing the flesh. This will enable the fat to be rendered as the meat cooks.

Heat a large sauté pan or skillet over medium heat and add the breasts, skin-side down. Cook until the skin on the bottom is crisp and brown, about 8 to 10 minutes. Turn and cook on the opposite side for a minute or two; the meat should be just slightly pink. Cut the duck breasts into thin slices, ladle the sauce over, and serve immediately.

**SERVES 6 AS A MAIN COURSE**

TOM AND GIANA FERGUSON MAKE GUBBEEN, ONE of the finest Irish farmhouse cheeses, on an enchanted two-hundred-acre farm in County Cork that is a kind of open house for their family and friends. The seaside village of Schull, a mile away, is a draw for many discerning visitors from London and points farther removed. They come for the beauty of rock, bog, and sea, and a warm welcome that makes up for the chill of the winter rains.

They come, too, for artisanal foods that have maintained their wholesome and delicious quality: hearth-baked quick breads made from fresh-milled whole-wheat flour, vegetables with the flavor of the salt and minerals from the sea-nourished soil, salmon of just-caught freshness, and especially cheeses.

A high-spirited and well-traveled young woman who moved to the country when she married a fifth-generation farmer, Giana began making Gubbeen (the name comes from the Gaelic word *goibín,* meaning "little mouth") with milk from her husband's family farm. Irish cow's milk is still among Europe's best flavored, and few other people in the country make washed-rind, semisoft-style cheeses. The cheese, with its own nutty sweetness, caught on with guests, and the couple started selling it locally and internationally.

Visitors to the Fergusons' farm come not just for the fresh and smoked Gubbeen but also for the home-cured bacon and Spanish-style sausages that the Fergusons' son, Fingal, cures from family pigs. Most of all they come for the charm of the family. The vibrant Giana heads an active local Slow Food chapter, or convivium, and shares her inbred understanding of country food and life with brimming good humor.

# BAKED CHEESE WITH WINTER HERBS

*Gubbeen is a big, semisoft, lightly tangy cow's milk cheese that lends itself to this "dead simple" recipe, as Giana says, for baked cheese. It's more interesting than the standard baked Brie for its hit of fresh resinous herbs and its daring—for Ireland, at least—hint of garlic.*

❊ ❊ ❊ ❊ ❊ ❊ ❊ ❊

1-pound wheel semisoft
    cheese, such as Gubbeen,
    Reblochon, or Port Salut

1 tablespoon minced mixed
    fresh herbs, such as thyme
    and rosemary
2 cloves garlic, minced

Freshly ground black pepper
    to taste
Crusty loaf of bread for serving

❊ ❊ ❊ ❊ ❊ ❊ ❊ ❊

Preheat the oven to 325°F. Cut the cheese in half horizontally to make 2 rounds. Sprinkle the herbs, garlic, and black pepper on the bottom half of the cheese. Replace the top disk of cheese and place the wheel on a large piece of aluminum foil. Wrap the foil around the cheese, forming a chimney hole on top with the excess foil. The chimney will let out the moisture while the cheese bakes. Place the cheese on a baking sheet and bake for 20 minutes, or until the cheese is soft and runny.

Spread on slices or chunks of bread while the cheese is still warm.

**SERVES 6 AS A FIRST COURSE**

# YUM, YUM, PIGS BUM

*Giana says that the delightful name for this soup comes from a children's skipping song that goes "Yum, yum, pig's bum, cabbage and potataaaaaaas!" Along with* Gascon *garbure (page 99), it shows the universality of cabbage-and-potato soup. It's even easier, requiring almost no preparation and not much cooking time. Here, the flavor comes from crisped bacon or garlic sausage, and the potatoes are roughly puréed to give the soup a thick, hearty texture.*

❊ ❊ ❊ ❊ ❊ ❊ ❊ ❊ ❊

12 ounces dark green kale, such as dinosaur or lacinato
6 cups water
Salt to taste

1 pound russet potatoes, peeled and cut into ½-inch dice
¼ cup extra-virgin olive oil
Freshly ground black pepper to taste

4 ounces smoked garlic sausage, cut into ½-inch dice, or smoked bacon, cut into ¼-inch crosswise slices

❊ ❊ ❊ ❊ ❊ ❊ ❊ ❊ ❊

Strip the cabbage leaves from their stems and cut away the tough mid-ribs of any large leaves. Roll the leaves tightly into cigars and, using a sharp knife, cut them into shreds. Set aside.

In a medium saucepan, bring the water to a boil and add salt. Add the potatoes and cook until soft and beginning to fall apart, about 8 to 10 minutes. Using a potato masher, smash them into a purée. Adjust the heat so that the soup simmers gently. Add the cabbage, olive oil, and salt and black pepper, keeping in mind

that the sausage or bacon may be salty. Simmer until the cabbage is tender, 6 to 8 minutes.

Meanwhile, cook the sausage or bacon in a sauté pan or skillet over medium heat until crisp and golden brown. Drain the fat and set the meat aside.

Ladle the soup into warmed bowls. Divide the sausage or bacon among the bowls.

**SERVES 4 TO 6 AS A MAIN COURSE**

# WHOLEMEAL WEST CORK SCONES FROM ADELÉ'S CAFÉ

*Adelé Conner is, Giana Ferguson claims, "one of the best bakers in Ireland."
That's awfully high praise for a nation that considers wholemeal quick breads
second only in sacredness to potatoes. Giana is lucky to live near Adelé's bakery,
and to have access to the same soft whole-wheat flour she uses, from Donal
Creadon, one of the country's few remaining small millers. You can get results
almost as good from whole-wheat pastry flour. ✳ These are moderately rich, very
short scones that remain soft and warm inside while forming a bit of a crust.
They're best right out of the oven, but take to toasting. Note an important
absence in the ingredients: sugar. They aren't at all sweet, meaning they can go
with a cheese—say, the Fergusons' Gubbeen—or smoked salmon. Or you can be
staunchly British and follow the baker's taste: Conner prefers her scones with
proper strawberry jam and whipped cream.*

✳ ✳ ✳ ✳ ✳ ✳ ✳ ✳

2 1/3 cups stone-ground whole-wheat pastry flour
3/4 cup all-purpose flour

1 teaspoon salt
2 teaspoons baking soda
1/2 cup (1 stick) cold unsalted butter, cut into small pieces

About 1 1/2 cups buttermilk
1 egg
1 tablespoon heavy cream

✳ ✳ ✳ ✳ ✳ ✳ ✳ ✳

Preheat the oven to 450°F. In a large bowl, combine the flours, salt, and baking soda. Stir to blend. Add the butter. Using a pastry blender, 2 knives, or your fingertips, quickly cut or squeeze the butter into the flour until it's the size of small peas. Add just enough buttermilk so that the mixture holds together. Be careful not to overmix the dough.

Gather the dough into a ball and put it on a lightly floured work surface. Roll out or press the dough into a 1 1/2-inch-thick mass. Cut the dough into rounds using a 3-inch round biscuit cutter. Press the excess dough together and cut again. Whisk together the egg and cream in a small bowl to make a wash. Brush over the scones. Put the scones on a baking sheet and bake until they are brown and sound hollow when tapped, about 20 minutes.

**MAKES 6 SCONES**

**STEVE JOHNSON**
*The Blue Room*
*Cambridge*
**MASSACHUSETTS**

STEVE JOHNSON IS ONE OF AMERICA'S LEADING CHEFS in forging alliances with local farms and urging his fellow chefs to do the same. He's also a cook with the rare combination of instinctive and careful attention to the foods of his own town and the places he has visited.

Soon after becoming chef and owner of The Blue Room, his very lively Cambridge bistro, Johnson started working with local farms, asking them to plant herbs and vegetables no one else did. He enlisted fellow cooks to buy the farms' produce, too, so the farmers would see that this was more than a passing experiment. Economic support and renovation of heritage crops is just what Slow Food does in its Presidia; Johnson went his own way, gathering a group of like-minded young cooks to support farmers who use sustainable techniques. Calling themselves the Chef's Collaborative, these cooks, from all over the country, take stands on environmental issues of the day.

Johnson spends several weeks each year in Costa Rica. His explorations of local foods there have brought color to his menu. At The Blue Room he brings to life the traditions of New England cookery through the use of the farm-raised ingredients he puts into every dish.

# FRIED PLANTAINS WITH CHIPOTLE KETCHUP

*This appetizer sells out every night at The Blue Room. You'll see why when you try the easy "ketchup," sweet and spicy and addictive. It's just as good with grilled and barbecued meats as it is with fried plantains, with their crisp outsides and soft, slightly sweet flesh.*

✳ ✳ ✳ ✳ ✳ ✳ ✳ ✳ ✳

**CHIPOTLE KETCHUP:**
One 12-ounce can plum
   tomatoes, without juice
1 tablespoon canola oil
½ onion, cut into ¼-inch dice
1½ teaspoons ground coriander

Salt to taste
2 tablespoons packed brown
   sugar
2 dried chipotle chilies, seeded
   and minced

1½ teaspoons tomato paste
2 tablespoons cider vinegar

4 to 6 plantains (1 per person)
1 tablespoon canola oil, plus
   more as needed

✳ ✳ ✳ ✳ ✳ ✳ ✳ ✳ ✳

TO MAKE THE KETCHUP: In a blender or food processor, purée the plum tomatoes. Strain through a fine-mesh sieve. Set aside.

Heat the oil in a medium sauté pan or skillet over medium heat. Add the onion, coriander, and a generous pinch of salt, and sauté until the onion is translucent, about 3 minutes. Add the brown sugar and cook for 2 more minutes. Add the tomato purée, chipotles, tomato paste, and vinegar. Reduce the heat to low and gently simmer, stirring occasionally, until the ketchup thickens, about 30 minutes. Purée the cooked

ketchup with a mixer or in the food processor or blender. Taste and adjust the seasoning, if necessary. Set aside to cool.

Peel and cut the plantains into 1¼-inch-thick slices. Heat 1 tablespoon of the oil in a medium sauté pan or skillet over medium heat. Fry the plantains in small batches until golden brown on both sides, about 5 minutes (you may need to add more oil to the pan if it becomes dry). Serve warm, with the chipotle ketchup in a ramekin on the side.

**SERVES 4 TO 6 AS A FIRST COURSE**

# COD BRAISED WITH WHITE WINE, POTATOES, AND ESCAROLE

*Boston was ever the land of the bean and the cod, and Steve Johnson honors that heritage with this straightforward and very good fish stew. It also shows off salt cod, long an Atlantic staple and increasingly an ingredient chefs turn to for its pliant texture and unmistakable flavor.*

❊ ❊ ❊ ❊ ❊ ❊ ❊ ❊ ❊

1 pound salt cod, cut into small pieces
8 cups water
2 cups dry white wine
1 cup, plus 2 tablespoons olive oil
1 onion, thinly sliced

4 russet potatoes, peeled and cut into ¼-inch-thick half-rounds
4 cloves garlic, minced
1 teaspoon minced fresh thyme
2 leeks (white part only), thinly sliced and rinsed
Leaves from 1 head escarole, torn into ½-inch pieces

Salt to taste
2 pounds boneless, skinless fresh cod fillets, cut into eight 4-ounce portions
Freshly ground black pepper to taste
1 lemon (optional)
8 wedges bread, toasted

❊ ❊ ❊ ❊ ❊ ❊ ❊ ❊ ❊

Soak the salt cod for 1 hour in cold water to cover, changing the water at least 2 times before using. Drain.

In a soup pot, combine the salt cod, the 8 cups water, wine, the 1 cup olive oil, the onion, potatoes, garlic, and thyme. Bring to a simmer over medium heat and cook for 15 minutes. Add the leeks and escarole. Continue to simmer until all of the ingredients are tender, about 40 minutes. Taste the stew and season with salt, if necessary. Set aside.

Heat the 2 tablespoons olive oil in a large Dutch oven over medium-high heat. Sauté the cod fillets until golden brown on the bottom,

5 to 7 minutes. Turn the fish and add the salt cod stew. When the liquid comes to a simmer, cover and reduce the heat to low. Simmer until the fresh cod is opaque throughout, 2 to 3 minutes. There should be plenty of broth; if too much of the liquid has evaporated, add a splash of water.

Ladle the stew into warmed shallow bowls and float a cod fillet in each bowl. Sprinkle with black pepper and add a squeeze of lemon juice, if you like. Serve with a wedge of toasted bread to soak up the broth.

**SERVES 8 AS A MAIN COURSE**

# Mesclun Greens with Sherry Vinaigrette

*Very simple, yes, but as with his chipotle ketchup, Steve Johnson sells as much of this salad as he can make—perhaps because his greens come from a local farm with a greenhouse that supplies him year-round. It's easy to make this mustard-and-thyme vinaigrette, lightly sweet from the sherry vinegar, your daily dressing.*

❊ ❊ ❊ ❊ ❊ ❊ ❊ ❊ ❊

**SHERRY VINAIGRETTE:**
2 tablespoons sherry vinegar
1 small shallot, thinly sliced
¼ teaspoon Dijon mustard
¼ teaspoon whole-grain
 mustard

Leaves from 1 sprig thyme,
 minced
Salt to taste
2 tablespoons extra-virgin
 olive oil

3 tablespoons vegetable oil

6 small handfuls baby salad
 greens
Salt and freshly ground black
 pepper to taste

❊ ❊ ❊ ❊ ❊ ❊ ❊ ❊ ❊

TO MAKE THE VINAIGRETTE: In a small bowl, whisk the vinegar, shallot, mustards, thyme, and a pinch of salt together. Let the ingredients macerate for 10 minutes. Whisk in the oils. Taste and adjust the seasoning, if necessary.

Just before serving, put the greens in a large bowl, season lightly with salt and black pepper, and gently toss with the vinaigrette to coat the greens lightly. Serve immediately.

**SERVES 4 TO 6 AS A FIRST COURSE**

ANA SORTUN MAKES WONDROUS-FLAVORED FOOD at her Oleana Restaurant in Cambridge, Massachusetts. Her distinctive name—Oleana is her full first name—is Norwegian, and she looks unmistakably Nordic. She has cooked food from all parts of Italy and France in her time as a cheerful, popular chef in and around Boston.

But Sortun's heart, and her palate, are somewhere mid-Balkans with a distinct loyalty to Turkey, where she has spent weeks at a time in small villages known for the quality of their cooking. The cultural anthropologist in her soul, and the inbred cooking ability in her hands, had already given her an impressive repository of recipes from southern Italy, Morocco, and Tunisia.

Sortun was able to soak up the spirit of the Turkish women cooks who hosted her in Gaziantep, a small city in southeastern Turkey that has been posited as the site of the Garden of Eden. Now, at her own Oleana Restaurant, she imports ingredients like sweet and hot red Maras peppers and various herbs no one else gets. And she seeks out local farmers. Her aim is to bring Americans a taste of the food the women lovingly shared—food that had sustained their families for centuries.

# LAMB STEAK WITH TURKISH SPICES AND FAVA BEAN MOUSSAKA

*This spectacular lamb dish was conceived for a fully staffed restaurant kitchen or a village filled with women helping one another. You'll want to make note of the authoritatively spiced marinade, gently sweet and hot, to use on any cut of lamb, grilled as here or roasted; it's great for barbecues, too. You can double the recipe and store the marinade for several weeks in the refrigerator. ❋ The moussaka, with its bed of potato and fava-bean purée, rolls of lamb-stuffed eggplant, and yogurt-spiked Mornay sauce, is a weekend project. It's rich, more sweet than spicy, and a true taste of the complex, plush family food of the Middle East.*

❋ ❋ ❋ ❋ ❋ ❋ ❋ ❋ ❋

One 2½-pound lamb roast, preferably top of leg of lamb, cut into eight 5-ounce steaks
Salt and freshly ground black pepper to taste

**SPICE PASTE:**
½ red bell pepper, seeded, deribbed, and coarsely chopped
2 tablespoons Aleppo chilies, fresh ground red chilies, or paprika powder
2 tablespoons tomato paste
¼ cup canola or olive oil
1 clove garlic, minced

1½ teaspoons dried oregano
1 teaspoon ground cinnamon
1 teaspoon ground nutmeg
1 teaspoon ground cumin
1 teaspoon ground coriander
2 teaspoons dried mint
2 teaspoons ground pepper

Fava Bean Moussaka (recipe follows)

❋ ❋ ❋ ❋ ❋ ❋ ❋ ❋ ❋

Season the lamb steaks with a generous amount of salt and black pepper. Set aside.

TO MAKE THE PASTE: In a blender, purée the bell pepper. In a small sauté pan or skillet, cook the purée over medium heat until it forms a thick concentrate. Remove from the heat and set aside.

In a small bowl, combine the pepper purée and all the remaining spice paste ingredients. Rub the paste on the lamb, cover, and refrigerate overnight.

Remove the lamb from the refrigerator. Light a fire in a charcoal grill. Grill the lamb over medium-hot coals for 4 to 6 minutes on each side for medium-rare. Transfer to a cutting board and loosely cover with aluminum foil. Let rest for 10 minutes. Cut the lamb against the grain into thin slices and serve with fava bean moussaka.

**SERVES 8 AS A MAIN COURSE**

# Fava Bean Moussaka

2 russet potatoes, peeled and
   cut into large chunks
2 pounds fava beans, shelled
2 tablespoons extra-virgin
   olive oil
Salt to taste
1 tablespoon unsalted butter
1 pound ground lamb
1 onion, cut into ¼-inch dice
1 clove garlic
1 tablespoon tomato paste

1 teaspoon ground cinnamon
⅓ cup golden raisins
1 cup canned chopped
   tomatoes
⅓ cup minced fresh flat-leaf
   parsley
2 tablespoons minced fresh
   mint
2 large globe eggplants, cut
   into ¼-inch-thick
   crosswise slices

**MORNAY SAUCE:**
2 cups milk
¼ white onion
1 clove
1 bay leaf
4 tablespoons unsalted butter
¼ cup all-purpose flour
Pinch of ground nutmeg
¾ cup kasseri cheese
¾ cup plain yogurt, preferably
   sheep's milk

❋ ❋ ❋ ❋ ❋ ❋ ❋ ❋

Cook the potatoes in lightly salted boiling water until tender, 8 to 10 minutes. Drain. Press through a ricer or mash thoroughly. Put the potatoes in a medium bowl and set aside.

Cook the fava beans in boiling water for 3 minutes. Drain and immediately plunge them into ice-cold water to cool. Pierce the outer skin of each bean with your thumbnail and pinch the bean out of its skin. In a food processor, combine the favas and extra-virgin olive oil. Purée until smooth and creamy. Add the fava bean purée to the potatoes and fold to combine. Season with salt and set aside.

Melt the butter in a medium sauté pan or skillet over medium-high heat. Add the ground lamb and a generous pinch of salt. Sauté until the lamb is lightly browned. Add the onion, garlic, tomato paste, cinnamon, and raisins. Reduce the heat to medium-low and cook until the onion begins to soften, about 5 minutes. Add the tomatoes and continue to cook until the most of the liquid has evaporated, about 10 minutes. Stir in the parsley and mint, season with salt, and set aside.

Preheat the oven to 450°F. Coat 2 baking sheets with olive oil. Top each sheet with a single layer of eggplant slices and season with salt. Roast the eggplant until soft, about 12 minutes.

Remove from the oven and set aside, leaving the oven on.

MEANWHILE, TO MAKE THE MORNAY SAUCE: In a small saucepan, combine the milk, onion, clove, and bay leaf. Bring to a very low simmer over low heat and cook for 10 minutes. Using a slotted spoon, remove the onion, clove, and bay leaf.

Melt the butter in a medium saucepan over medium heat. Whisk in the flour. Whisking constantly, cook the mixture for 1 minute. Gradually whisk in the warm milk mixture. Continue to whisk and cook over medium heat until the mixture thickens, about 1 minute. Add the nutmeg and cheese and whisk again until the cheese melts and the mixture is smooth. Remove from the heat and stir in the yogurt. Set aside.

To assemble, reduce the oven temperature to 400°F. In a 9-by-15-inch baking dish, spread the fava bean mixture in an even layer. Spoon about 2 tablespoons of the lamb mixture onto each slice of eggplant and roll up. Place the eggplant rolls on top of the purée and pour the Mornay sauce on top. Bake in the oven until the sauce begins to bubble, about 15 minutes.

**SERVES 8 AS A MAIN COURSE**

# FIDEOS WITH SPECIAL CHICKPEAS AND SAFFRON

*Fideos, toasted angel-hair pasta simmered in broth, appear wherever Spanish influence is strongly felt, from Catalonia and Sardinia to Cuba and Central America. Here, the broth is exotically scented with the New World gifts of cocoa, vanilla, and ancho chilies, and with the Spanish hallmark of saffron. Thickened with chickpea purée and served with chard and a potent aioli, this is a one-dish meal.*

2 cups dried chickpeas, soaked in water overnight and drained, or 3½ cups canned chickpeas, drained
Salt to taste
1 tablespoon canola oil
1 onion, coarsely chopped
1 carrot, peeled and chopped
4 cloves garlic, minced

1 bay leaf
½ vanilla bean, halved lengthwise
1 teaspoon saffron threads
1 teaspoon ground coriander seed
1 teaspoon ground fennel seed
1 tablespoon unsweetened cocoa powder

1 ancho chile, stemmed and seeded
4 cups chopped canned tomatoes
8 cups water
1 pound dried angel hair pasta
¼ cup extra-virgin olive oil
1 pound green chard, stemmed and chopped
Aioli (page 117)

If using dried chickpeas, put them in a soup pot and cover with water by 1 inch. Bring to a simmer and season with salt. Gently simmer the chickpeas until tender, adding more water as necessary to keep them covered with liquid, 1 to 2 hours depending on the age of the chickpeas. Drain and set aside.

Meanwhile, heat the canola oil in a soup pot over medium heat and sauté the onion, carrot, and a generous pinch of salt until the onion is translucent, about 3 minutes. Add the garlic and sauté for 1 minute. Add the bay leaf, vanilla bean, saffron, coriander seed, fennel seed, cocoa, chile, tomatoes, and water. Increase the heat to medium-high and bring to a simmer. Cook to reduce by one-third, about 30 minutes. Remove the vanilla bean and bay leaf, discarding the bay leaf and reserving the vanilla bean. In a blender, purée the broth and vegetables. Strain the purée through a fine-mesh sieve. Scrape the vanilla seeds from the bean (if they have not already fallen into the simmering broth) and add. You should have about 5 cups. Taste and adjust the seasoning, if necessary.

Preheat the oven to 350°F. Spread the pasta in an even layer on a baking sheet and toast in the oven until golden brown, about 10 minutes. Remove from the oven and let cool. Break the pasta into 2-inch pieces.

Heat the olive oil in a soup pot over medium heat. Add the chard and cook until wilted. Add the vegetable broth and bring to a simmer. Add the chickpeas and toasted pasta. Simmer until the broth has been absorbed and the noodles are tender. Just before serving, stir in ¾ cup of the aioli and season with salt, if necessary.

**SERVES 6 AS A MAIN COURSE**

# AIOLI

2 small cloves garlic, coarsely
  chopped
Salt to taste

2 egg yolks
1 teaspoon Dijon mustard
Grated zest of 2 lemons

1 tablespoon fresh lemon juice
1½ cups extra-virgin olive oil

❁ ❁ ❁ ❁ ❁ ❁ ❁ ❁ ❁

With a mortar and pestle or the flat blade of a knife, mash the garlic and a pinch of salt into a smooth paste. Set aside.

In a small bowl, whisk the yolks, mustard, and lemon zest and juice together. Whisk in the oil drop by drop until the mixture begins to emulsify and thicken; then gradually increase the flow while whisking. When all of the oil has been added, stir in the garlic and season with salt, if necessary.

**MAKES 2 CUPS**

LIKE ALL GREAT CHEFS, DANIEL BOULUD USES THE most sophisticated and rarefied techniques to achieve simplicity and make dishes taste authoritatively of what's in them. Before beautiful presentation, before exotic and rare ingredients, the food must taste good. Boulud's food always does.

Boulud learned about simple and good cooking at the roadside café and "not-quite restaurant" that his great-grandparents, grandparents, and then parents ran on the family farm in St. Pierre-de-Chandieu, a village near Lyon. This was a place, he says, where "people went to begin and finish a day, to toast births and marriages and to mourn losses. It was where love affairs started and, of course, where some ended. It was warm, welcoming, and a vital part of village life."

Growing and serving food was in Boulud's blood. So was an ambition that led him to apprentice with starred chefs in and around Lyon, to win international prizes even as a very young chef, and to establish a legendary reputation in New York City, where his restaurant Daniel is considered the best in an intensely competitive city.

Many diners prefer the smaller Café Boulud, named for his family's roadside farm café, in the smaller Manhattan quarters of the first Daniel. There, Boulud serves seasonal food often taken from his childhood—living rural history in a relentlessly modern city.

# BARBOTON D'ANGEAU

*This simple and satisfying lamb stew is straight from Daniel Boulud's Dauphinois childhood. It's the kind of economical and tasty supper that remains so close to his heart that when the French government decorated Boulud, he served a citified version of it to his family and friends to celebrate the honor. The fancy version, Agneau Champvallon, uses lamb chops; the humbler original, the one his grandmother cooked on a weeknight, uses shoulder—cheaper, better for a stew—and big chunks of potato that break off into the sauce and thicken it. ✳ One story of the unusual name is that it honors the feast of Saint Barbara, patron saint of miners and artillerymen. Saint Barbara protects against lightning, a hazard in both professions. A Turkish-born medieval martyr, she was locked by her father in a tower to prevent her from becoming Christian. After learning that she had been baptized in secret, he beheaded her and was immediately struck by lightning. ✳ Away from home, workmen and soldiers often had to cook for themselves, and a lamb stew was within anyone's reach. In Dauphinois households—Boulud's native village was officially in the Dauphiné before the French government redistricted it into the region of Lyon in the early 1960s—the flavoring was often the leftover pan juices from a Sunday roast.*

✳ ✳ ✳ ✳ ✳ ✳ ✳ ✳ ✳

3 pounds boneless lamb shoulder, trimmed of fat and cut into 2-inch chunks
Flour for dusting
Salt and freshly ground black pepper to taste
4 tablespoons unsalted butter
2 large onions (1 pound total), cut into ½-inch wedges
2 leeks (½ pound total), including white and pale green parts only, rinsed, and cut into ½-inch slices
2 cloves garlic, minced
1 cup dry white wine, preferably Chardonnay
3 pounds Yukon Gold or other yellow-fleshed potatoes, peeled and quartered or cut into 1-inch cubes, reserved in cold water
6 to 8 cups unsalted chicken stock or water
2 sprigs fresh thyme, preferably wild *(serpolet)*
2 sprigs winter savory
1 bay leaf
Leaves from 2 sprigs flat-leaf parsley, minced
*Fleur de sel*, for finishing

✳ ✳ ✳ ✳ ✳ ✳ ✳ ✳ ✳

Preheat the oven to 350°F. Place an oven rack in the center of the oven.

Lightly dust the lamb with the flour and season with salt and black pepper. In an enameled cast-iron Dutch oven or a heavy ovenproof casserole, melt 2 tablespoons of the butter over medium-high heat. Add the lamb and brown for 6 to 10 minutes. Add the remaining 2 tablespoons butter and sweat the onions, leeks, and garlic along with the browned meat over medium heat until the vegetables are translucent, 8 to 10 minutes. Make sure that they do not color. Add the wine and cook to reduce the liquid by three-fourths. Add the potatoes and stock or water, making sure that the lamb and vegetables are covered by 1 to 2 inches of liquid. Add the thyme, savory, and bay leaf and stir well to incorporate. Cover the pot loosely with a lid or with an oiled or buttered round of parchment paper pricked with a tiny air hole in the center.  Return to a boil and transfer the pot to the oven.

Bake the stew until the lamb is very tender and the potatoes are soft and have begun to break up, so that they thicken the sauce, 1½ to 2 hours; cook for up to 30 minutes longer, if necessary. Discard the parchment, if used, and add the thyme, savory, and bay leaf.

Ladle the stew into shallow rim soup bowls and sprinkle with parsley just before serving. Serve with pepper and *fleur de sel* on the side.

**SERVES 4 TO 6 AS A MAIN COURSE**

## CREAMED SPINACH (CRÈME D'EPINARDS)

*The spinach is a homey everyday dish with an ingenious* truc: *a simple but intensely flavored puréed cream mixed into the blanched leaf spinach, flavoring it all and keeping the color a brilliant green.*

| | | |
|---|---|---|
| 4 pounds spinach, stemmed and tough mid-ribs removed | ½ cup chopped onion | 1 cup heavy cream |
| 2 teaspoons unsalted butter | 1 teaspoon minced garlic | Salt and freshly ground black pepper to taste |
| | Pinch of ground nutmeg | |

Blanch the spinach in a large pot of salted boiling water for 2 to 3 minutes. Drain, rinse under cold running water, transfer to a colander, and press with the back of a large spoon to remove any excess moisture.

In a medium sauté pan or skillet over medium heat, melt the butter. Add the onion and garlic and cook until translucent, about 3 minutes. Add the nutmeg, cream, and 1 pound of the blanched spinach leaves. Season with salt and pepper. Cook until the spinach is lightly tender, about 4 to 5 minutes. In a blender or food processor, purée the cream mixture.

In a medium saucepan, combine the remaining blanched spinach and the spinach purée. Season with salt and black pepper. Cook until lightly thickened. Serve immediately.

**SERVES 4 TO 6 AS A SIDE DISH**

BEN AND KAREN BARKER TAKE A LOVING AND SCHOL-
arly approach to the food of the American South at their
Magnolia Grill, in Durham, North Carolina. Southern food
is famous for its down-home richness—biscuits and fat-filled
gravy, greens cooked with ham bones, the rustic dishes called "soul food."

Much less well known is the delicacy of a cuisine that strongly reflects the African-
Americans who were ever the repositories of kitchen wisdom. Slaves brought with them an
extremely subtle combination of African spicing and French technique, filtered through
the Caribbean. Many books have detailed the underappreciated refinement of this cuisine,
which relies on complete freshness and simplicity to highlight flavors; among the best advo-
cates are Karen Hess (*The Carolina Rice Kitchen,* University of South Carolina Press) and John
Martin Taylor (*Hoppin' John's Lowcountry Cooking,* Houghton Mifflin).

The Barkers read up on and celebrate this history at their restaurant, looking
for ways to translate a little-known heritage into dishes that combine subtlety and powerful
flavor. They find ways to use salty, dry country ham, for instance, as an accent, rather than as
a dully overpowering main ingredient. And they don't hesitate to use the power of peppers
and onions—as integral to the South as country ham.

# TOMATO SOUP WITH POACHED EGG AND SERRANO HAM

*This Creole-influenced, mildly piquant soup serves as a one-dish meal. If you have North Carolina country ham, be sure to use it.*

❊ ❊ ❊ ❊ ❊ ❊ ❊ ❊

¼ cup olive oil
4 ounces Serrano ham, cut into
    ¼-inch dice (about ⅔ cup)
1 onion, cut into ¼-inch dice
½ cup minced garlic
Generous pinch of red pepper
    flakes
1 bay leaf
1 tablespoon *pimenton* (Spanish
    smoked paprika)

3 pounds tomatoes, seeded and
    cut into 1-inch pieces
Salt to taste
2 tablespoons sherry vinegar
1 cup dry white wine
1 cup chicken stock
Freshly ground black pepper
    to taste
6 large eggs

**GARNISH:**
1½ cups bread cubes, tossed
    in olive oil and toasted
Chunk of Manchego cheese
Spanish extra-virgin olive oil
2 tablespoons coarsely
    chopped fresh tarragon

❊ ❊ ❊ ❊ ❊ ❊ ❊ ❊

Heat the olive oil in a medium nonreactive saucepan over medium heat. Add the ham and sauté until lightly browned. Using a slotted spoon, transfer the ham to a plate.

Add the onion and cook over medium heat until translucent, about 3 minutes. Add the garlic, red pepper flakes, bay leaf, and *pimenton* and cook for 1 minute. Add the tomatoes and a generous pinch of salt. Cook for 5 minutes, stirring frequently. Add 1 tablespoon vinegar, wine, and stock. Bring to a simmer and cook gently for 10 to 15 minutes.

Remove the bay leaf and pass the tomato mixture through the fine blade of a food mill or push through a coarse-mesh sieve with the back of a large spoon. Adjust the consistency

with stock or water if necessary, and season with salt and black pepper. Set aside and keep warm.

In a medium nonreactive sauté pan or skillet, bring 4 inches of water to a boil and reduce heat to the barest simmer. Add the remaining vinegar and poach the eggs, 2 at a time, until the white part has set but the yolk is still quite runny. Using a slotted spoon, transfer each egg to a warmed soup bowl as it is cooked.

Divide the cooked ham among the bowls. Ladle the hot soup around the eggs and sprinkle the croutons on top. With a vegetable peeler, shave the cheese over each bowl. Drizzle the cheese with olive oil, sprinkle with tarragon, and serve.

**SERVES 4 AS A FIRST COURSE**

# Roasted Fresh Ham with Salsa Verde

*The Barkers' motto at Magnolia Grill is Not Afraid of Flavor. They defy America's sadly bland pork, bred to reassure those afraid of both fat and flavor, with this marinade for roasting. The pungent* salsa verde, *with the citrus fragrance of lemon verbena leaves (if you can find them), again nods to the Creole influence apparent in the Carolinas.*

1 cup packed fresh cilantro leaves
½ cup roasted garlic purée
4 jalapeño chilies, seeded and minced
½ cup olive oil
2½ tablespoons kosher salt
One 8-pound fresh bone-in ham or pork shoulder
Salsa Verde (recipe follows)

In a small bowl, combine the cilantro, garlic, chilies, olive oil, and salt. Stir to blend. Rub all over the ham or pork. Cover and refrigerate overnight.

Remove the meat from the refrigerator about 1½ hours before roasting and place on a rack set in a roasting pan.

Preheat the oven to 400°F. Roast the ham or pork for 45 minutes. Reduce the heat to 300°F and roast for 2 more hours, or until an instant-read thermometer inserted in the center of the meat registers 155°F. Remove from the oven, cover loosely with aluminum foil, and let rest for 25 to 30 minutes.

Cut the ham or pork across the grain into ⅓-inch-thick slices. Pass the salsa verde separately.

**SERVES 6 TO 8 AS A MAIN COURSE**

## Salsa Verde

4 cloves garlic
1 tablespoon capers, rinsed
1 salt-packed anchovy, filleted and rinsed
1 jalapeño chile, seeded and coarsely chopped
¼ cup packed fresh lemon verbena leaves, or ¼ cup packed fresh flat-leaf parsley leaves and grated zest of 1 lemon
¼ cup packed fresh cilantro leaves
½ cup olive oil
Salt to taste

In a mortar, pound the garlic, capers, anchovy, chile, lemon verbena leaves, and cilantro into a thick paste with a pestle. Stir in the olive oil and season with salt. Set aside at room temperature for up to 1 hour.

**MAKES 1 CUP**

# HOMINY SUCCOTASH

*Completely Southern, this is the kind of dish that field workers, whose main meal was at midday, would have as supper. Using both fresh corn and white hominy, it is an especially good, full-flavored version of an American classic whose homeland is the Barkers' backyard.*

✳ ✳ ✳ ✳ ✳ ✳ ✳ ✳ ✳

2 tablespoons olive oil
1 onion, cut into ¼-inch dice
1 red bell pepper, cut into
　　¼-inch dice
Salt to taste
4 cloves garlic, minced
Pinch of red pepper flakes
1 bay leaf

10 ounces thawed frozen lima
　　beans, or 2 pounds fresh
　　lima beans, shelled and
　　blanched for 2 minutes
About 1½ cups chicken stock
2 cups fresh corn kernels
　　(about 4 large ears corn)
16 ounces canned white
　　hominy, drained and rinsed

1½ cups heavy cream
2 tablespoons chopped fresh
　　flat-leaf parsley
2 teaspoons chopped fresh
　　marjoram
Freshly ground black pepper
　　to taste

✳ ✳ ✳ ✳ ✳ ✳ ✳ ✳ ✳

Heat the olive oil in a large sauté pan or skillet over medium heat. Add the onion, bell pepper, and a generous pinch of salt. Cook until the onion is translucent, about 5 minutes. Add the garlic, red pepper flakes, and bay leaf, and cook for 30 seconds. Add the lima beans and enough chicken broth to cover the vegetables. Bring to a simmer and cook until the limas are tender, 8 to 10 minutes. Add chicken stock if necessary to keep the beans covered while cooking.

Add the corn and simmer until tender, about 2 minutes. Remove from the heat and set aside.

In a small saucepan, combine the hominy and cream. Bring to a simmer over medium heat and cook until slightly thickened, 5 to 10 minutes. Stir the hominy and cream into the lima bean mixture and cook over low heat for a few minutes to heat through. Add the parsley, marjoram, and season with salt and black pepper.

**SERVES 6 TO 8 AS A SIDE DISH**

**RICK BAYLESS**

*Topolobampo and Frontera Grill*

*Chicago*

**ILLINOIS**

RICK BAYLESS MAKES THE BEST MEXICAN FOOD north of the border—even better than in Mexico, many unsentimental experts say.

Bayless is far too gracious even to countenance such a notion, but he will admit to an undying passion for the food of Mexico as it is cooked and lived. He grew up in Oklahoma City, with a barbecue restaurant in his family. A high-school field trip to Mexico was his conversion experience: this country and this culture would be his life's work.

He studied Spanish and Latin American culture at the University of Michigan, where he met his wife, Deann. The couple began catering to support themselves, and that turned into the career in which they have been full partners.

Had Slow Food USA existed then, the Baylesses would have been charter members: they have been just the kind of activists and teachers who have built Slow Food. Instead, they have established their own empire. Frontera Grill, the storefront restaurant they opened in Chicago, became one of the city's most popular restaurants from the first day. Here is where people can find tacos, salsa, and tortillas kneaded and baked on a hot iron plate the way women in Mexico make them. Next door to Frontera Grill, the couple opened Topolobampo, a quieter restaurant with a fuller menu of subtly flavored, completely hand-made dishes from various regions of Mexico, especially their favored Oaxaca. They transmitted their scholarly love of Mexico in a landmark book, *Authentic Mexican* (Scribner), which grew into a popular series of books.

# TORTILLA SOUP WITH PASILLA CHILIES, FRESH CHEESE, AND AVOCADO

*Here's a recipe, adapted from* Mexico—One Plate at a Time *(Scribner), that illustrates why Rick Bayless is not only one of the most popular chefs in America but also one of the most popular cookbook writers. Everyone loves the process of making this soup, from frying the tortillas to adding the condiments. Be sure to look for good cheese; if you can manage homemade chicken stock, you'll be getting very close to the cooking that inspires the Baylesses.*

❋ ❋ ❋ ❋ ❋ ❋ ❋ ❋ ❋

6 corn tortillas, halved
Canola oil for frying
4 cloves garlic, peeled and left whole
1 small white onion, sliced
2 pasilla chilies or 1 ancho chile, stemmed, seeded, and torn into several pieces

One 15-ounce can whole tomatoes in juice, drained, or 12 ounces tomatoes, cored and coarsely chopped
6 cups unsalted chicken stock, preferably homemade
1 large sprig epazote (optional)
½ teaspoon salt or to taste
6 ounces queso fresco or other crumbly fresh cheese such

as salted pressed farmer's cheese or feta, cut into ½-inch cubes; or 6 ounces soft white cheese, such as Chihuahua, quesillo, asadero, or Monterey jack, shredded
1 large avocado, peeled, pitted, and cut into ½-inch dice
1 large lime, cut into wedges

❋ ❋ ❋ ❋ ❋ ❋ ❋ ❋ ❋

Cut the tortillas vertically into ¼-inch-thick strips. In a medium saucepan, heat ½ inch oil over medium heat until it shimmers. The edge of a tortilla strip inserted in the oil should sizzle vigorously. Add half the tortilla strips. Stir until they are golden brown and crisp. With a slotted spoon, transfer to paper towels to drain. Repeat with the remaining tortillas.

Pour off all but a thin coating of hot oil and return the pan to the heat. Add the garlic and onion and cook, stirring frequently, until golden, about 7 minutes. Using a slotted spoon, press the garlic against the side of the pan to leave behind as much oil as possible, then transfer the garlic to a blender or food processor.

Add the chile pieces to the hot pan. Turn quickly as they fry, toast, and release a delicious aroma, about 30 seconds in all. (Too much frying/toasting will make them bitter.) Transfer to paper towels to drain. Set the pan aside.

Add the tomatoes to the blender or food processor and process to a smooth purée. If using fresh tomatoes, strain the purée to get rid of the pieces of tomato skin. Heat the same saucepan over medium-high heat. Add the tomato purée and stir until it has thickened to the consistency of tomato paste, about 10 minutes. Add the stock and epazote (if you like), bring to a boil, then partially cover and gently simmer over medium to medium-low heat for 30 minutes. Add the salt.

To serve, divide the cheese and avocado among warmed soup bowls. Ladle a portion of the broth into each bowl, top with a portion of the tortilla strips, and crumble on a little of the toasted chilies. Offer wedges of lime.

**SERVES 6 AS A FIRST COURSE, 4 AS A MAIN COURSE**

# TOMATILLO-BRAISED PORK LOIN

*"Rick's recipes are just plain good," says Tasha Prysi, the talented young chef who tested and perfected the recipes in this book. Here's an example, again from* Mexico—One Plate at a Time, *of what she means: a family dish that solves the too-lean American pork problem with garlic, herbs, and the acidic zing of fresh tomatillos. Tomatillos are essential, and roasting them and the chilies will wonderfully scent the kitchen.*

❋ ❋ ❋ ❋ ❋ ❋ ❋ ❋

1½ tablespoons pork lard, olive oil, or canola oil
One 2-pound boneless pork loin roast, untied if in 2 pieces

**TOMATILLO SAUCE:**
1 pound tomatillos, husked and rinsed

2 green jalapeño or serrano chilies
1 white onion, sliced
3 large cloves garlic, minced
1½ cups water
1 or 2 large sprigs epazote plus more for garnish, or ⅓ cup chopped fresh

cilantro, plus a few sprigs for garnish
1 teaspoon salt

10 small red boiling potatoes (about 1 pound total), scrubbed and quartered

❋ ❋ ❋ ❋ ❋ ❋ ❋ ❋

Preheat the oven to 325°F. In a large Dutch oven or heavy casserole, melt the lard or heat the oil over medium heat. Add the pork loin (if there is more than one piece, don't crowd them or they'll stew rather than brown) and brown well on the bottom, about 5 minutes. Turn the pork over and brown on the other side. Remove the pan from the heat and transfer the pork to a plate; set the pot aside to use for the sauce.

TO MAKE THE SAUCE: Preheat the broiler. Place the tomatillos and chilies on a baking sheet and roast them 4 inches from the heat source until dark brown with black spots, about 5 minutes. Flip the tomatillos and chilies over and roast on the other side until the tomatillos are splotchy black, blistered, and tender. Remove from the broiler and let cool. Transfer to a food processor or blender,

being careful to scrape up the juice that has run out onto the baking sheet, and purée until smooth.

Heat the Dutch oven or casserole over medium heat. Add the onion and cook, stirring frequently, until golden, about 7 minutes. Stir in the garlic and cook 1 minute longer. Raise the heat to medium-high and, when the ingredients begin to sizzle, add the tomatillo purée all at once. Stir until noticeably darker and very thick, 3 to 4 minutes. Add the water and 1 or 2 epazote sprigs or the chopped cilantro. Add the salt and stir thoroughly.

Place the browned pork into the warm sauce, cover the pot with a lid or aluminum foil, place in the oven, and cook for 30 minutes.

Meanwhile, cook the potatoes in heavily salted boiling water until tender, about 10 minutes.

Drain and set aside. After the pork has cooked for 30 minutes, add the potatoes. Re-cover and cook for about 10 minutes longer, or until an instant-read thermometer inserted into the center of the pork registers 145°F. The meat should feel rather firm but not hard and be very slightly pink in the center.

With a pair of tongs and a spatula, transfer the pork to a cutting board. Let it rest for 3 or 4 minutes while you finish the sauce: Spoon off any fat on the top of the sauce. Taste the sauce and adjust the seasoning, if necessary. Spoon the sauce and potatoes onto a warmed platter. Cut the pork into ¼-inch-thick slices and arrange them over the sauce. Decorate the platter with epazote or cilantro sprigs and serve.

**SERVES 6 AS A MAIN COURSE**

# BUTTERED CREPES WITH CARAMEL AND PECANS

*Adapted from* Authentic Mexican *(Scribner), this recipe is as close to crepes suzette as most of today's cooks are likely ever to get, and it's a lot more interesting. The batter is nicely spiced with cinnamon and cloves, and the filling— well, if you're one of the people who made dulce de leche Häagen-Dazs's most popular flavor introduction, you'll have to see how good caramelized milk can be when you make it yourself. Goat's milk gives flavor interest and balance to the sweetness, but don't hesitate to try this with cow's milk.*

✳ ✳ ✳ ✳ ✳ ✳ ✳ ✳ ✳

**CREPE BATTER:**
½-inch piece cinnamon stick, or ½ teaspoon ground cinnamon
3 whole cloves, or pinch of ground cloves
1 cup milk

2 large eggs
¼ teaspoon salt
1 teaspoon sugar
½ teaspoon vanilla extract
⅔ cup all-purpose flour
1 tablespoon unsalted butter, melted

Canola oil for frying
½ cup (1 stick) unsalted butter
1 cup coarsely chopped pecans
1½ cups Cajeta at room temperature (recipe follows)

✳ ✳ ✳ ✳ ✳ ✳ ✳ ✳ ✳

TO MAKE THE CREPE BATTER: In a mortar or spice grinder, pulverize the cinnamon and cloves. In a blender or food processor, combine the ground spices, milk, eggs, salt, sugar, vanilla, and flour. Process until smooth, stopping the machine once to scrape down the sides. With the machine running, pour in the melted butter. Set the batter aside at room temperature for 2 hours. Before using, thin the batter with a little water, if necessary; the consistency should resemble heavy cream.

To make the crepes, place a 7-inch skillet or crepe pan over medium to medium-high heat and brush very lightly with oil. When hot, pour in a scant ¼ cup batter, quickly swirl it in the pan to coat the bottom, and immediately pour the excess back into the blender or food processor jar. Cook until the edges begin to dry, 45 seconds to 1 minute. Loosen the edges with a knife and trim off the irregular part (where you poured off the excess batter). Using your fingers or a narrow spatula, flip

the crepe (it should be golden brown on the bottom). Cook until golden brown on the second side, about 1 minute, then transfer to a plate. Continue making crepes in the same manner, greasing the pan from time to time and stacking the finished crepes (there should be at least 12) on top of one another. Cover the crepes with plastic wrap and set aside.

To toast the pecans, melt the butter in a medium skillet over medium-low heat. Add the pecans and stir frequently until the nuts are toasted and the butter is browned, about 10 minutes. Using a slotted spoon, transfer to a bowl. Set the pan of browned butter aside.

Lay a crepe, prettiest-side down, on a work surface. Brush with the browned butter and spoon a scant 1 tablespoon *cajeta* on one side. Fold the crepe in half and press gently to spread out the filling. Brush the top with butter, fold in half to form a wedge, and brush with butter again. Lay the crepe in a buttered baking dish and repeat the process with the remaining crepes. Cover the dish with aluminum foil and scrape the remaining *cajeta* into a small saucepan. Set aside.

About 20 minutes before serving, preheat the oven to 325°F. Bake the crepes for 10 minutes to heat them through. Heat the remaining *cajeta* over medium-low heat. Drizzle it over the warm crepes, sprinkle with nuts, and serve at once.

**SERVES 4**

## CAJETA (GOAT'S MILK CARAMEL)

4 cups goat's milk
1 cup sugar
1 tablespoon corn syrup

½-inch piece cinnamon stick
¼ teaspoon baking soda
1 tablespoon water

1 tablespoon grain alcohol, sweet sherry, rum, or brandy

✳ ✳ ✳ ✳ ✳ ✳ ✳ ✳

In a large, heavy saucepan, combine the milk, sugar, corn syrup, and cinnamon. Bring to a simmer over medium heat, stirring constantly. Dissolve the baking soda in the water, remove the pan from the heat, and stir in the soda mixture; it will bubble up, so have a spoon ready to stir it down.

Return the pan to the heat and adjust the heat so the liquid simmers at a steady roll. Stir regularly as the mixture reduces. When the bubbles start changing from small, quick-bursting ones to larger, glassier ones, in 25 to 40 minutes, reduce the heat to medium-low. Stir frequently and thoroughly, washing the spoon afterward each time, until the mixture thickens into a caramel-colored syrup a little thinner than corn syrup.

To finish, strain the *cajeta* through a fine-mesh sieve into a small bowl or wide-mouthed jar. Let cool a few minutes, then stir in the alcohol. Let cool completely. Use immediately, or cover and refrigerate for up to 3 days.

**MAKES 3 CUPS**

DEBORAH MADISON IS A GURU TO COOKS WHO CARE about fresh, local food. She first came to prominence as the cook at Greens, a seminal vegetarian restaurant in San Francisco, and became a sort of greens goddess as the author of several definitive books on vegetarian cooking. Before her long and comprehensive books appeared, nonmeat eaters still had the reputation as eccentrics. With clear, sensible, and enticing recipes, she proves that vegetarians need miss none of the variety and life-enhancing sustenance of cooking.

The connection between farm and table is dear to Madison. She spent five years visiting hundreds of markets across the United States for her latest book, *Local Flavors* (Broadway Books). Slow Food founder Carlo Petrini often points to farmers' markets in the United States as paving the way for the rest of the world, which lags surprisingly far behind; Madison shows how and why.

The ideals of Slow Food, of course, resonate with Madison. Along with Chez Panisse founder Alice Waters, she has been a prime mover of Slow Food USA, using her considerable reputation as a proponent of good, fresh, seasonal food to enlist new adherents to the movement. As always, giving people ways to find and cook good food are the best lures.

# POSOLE WITH CHILE COLORADO

*Since moving to Santa Fe, Deborah Madison has become a devoted student of Native American crops and cooking. The short growing season of northern New Mexico, she explains, means that foods must be preserved. Corn, for instance, is slaked with lime to dissolve the outer layer of skin and then dried to produce a full-flavored posole. Ground, slaked corn becomes meal (masa), the basis for tamales. As with hominy, she says, the lime (potash) used in slaking "leaves the corn with an unusual flavor that's rich and somewhat nutty." Posole is usually cooked with pork or beef, but Madison loves the flavor of posole on its own. So she cooks posole with a sauce made from red or green chilies—"a must," she says, to add to its already robust flavor.*

❀ ❀ ❀ ❀ ❀ ❀ ❀ ❀ ❀

**CHILE COLORADO SAUCE:**
12 dried New Mexican chilies
3 cups boiling water
2 tablespoons canola oil
3 tablespoons finely chopped white onion
2 cloves garlic, minced
1 teaspoon ground cumin
½ teaspoon dried Mexican oregano
1½ tablespoons flour
¾ teaspoon salt

½ teaspoon distilled white vinegar, or to taste

**POSOLE:**
3 cups dried posole, soaked overnight
1 large onion, diced
3 cloves garlic, minced
1 tablespoon dried Mexican oregano
Pinch of dried thyme

2 teaspoons salt, plus more to taste
About 12 cups water or chicken stock

**GARNISH:**
Dried Mexican oregano
Diced onion
Finely shredded green cabbage
Chopped fresh cilantro
Lime wedges
Warm tortillas

❀ ❀ ❀ ❀ ❀ ❀ ❀ ❀ ❀

Preheat the oven to 200°F.

TO MAKE THE SAUCE: Discard the stems and seeds of the chilies and remove the veins. Place them on a baking sheet. Heat them in the oven with the door open for about 10 minutes, moving them around several times. Don't let them burn, or the sauce will be bitter.

Transfer the chilies to a bowl, add the boiling water, and let steep for 15 minutes. Using a slotted spoon, transfer to a blender or food processor. Add half of the soaking water. Purée for 2 minutes, or until smooth. Pour the purée

through a fine-mesh sieve into a bowl. Use the remaining soaking water to rinse out the blender, then add it to the purée. Add more water if the purée seems too thick.

Heat the oil in a medium saucepan over medium-low heat. Add the onion, garlic, cumin, and oregano. Cook, stirring frequently, until the onion colors lightly, about 5 minutes. Stir in the flour, then the chile purée. Cook over low heat, stirring frequently, for 15 minutes. Add the salt and stir in the vinegar.

TO MAKE THE POSOLE: Drain the posole. Put it in a soup pot and add the onion, garlic, oregano, thyme, and the 2 teaspoons salt. Pour in the water or stock; it should cover the posole. Simmer, uncovered, until tender but chewy, 2 to 3 hours. The time can vary widely, so start tasting for doneness after 1 hour. If the liquid cooks away, add more so that the posole ends up a bit soupy.

Stir in the chile sauce and season with salt. Serve the soup in warmed bowls, garnished with oregano, onion, cabbage, and cilantro. Serve the lime wedges alongside and eat with warm tortillas.

**SERVES 6 AS A MAIN COURSE**

# Cucumber and Purslane Salad with Sunflower Sprouts

*Deborah Madison devised this cooling salad to complement, and also to take some of the edge off, the heat of chile sauce. Cooling it is—and also typical of northern New Mexico, where fleshy-leaved purslane, an herb that is common throughout the Mediterranean, grows wild. The sunflower sprouts are for crunch. They're particularly nutty, but any sprouts will do nicely.*

❈ ❈ ❈ ❈ ❈ ❈ ❈ ❈

2 or 3 cucumbers, peeled
1½ cups purslane, sorrel, or watercress sprigs
3 green onions, including light green parts, slivered

2 tablespoons minced fresh flat-leaf parsley
1 tablespoon extra-virgin olive oil
Sea salt to taste

Fresh lime juice or champagne vinegar to taste (optional)
1 handful sunflower sprouts

❈ ❈ ❈ ❈ ❈ ❈ ❈ ❈

Halve the cucumbers lengthwise, scoop out the seeds, and chop into bite-sized pieces. Break the purslane, sorrel, or watercress sprigs into a medium bowl. Combine the green onions, cucumbers, and parsley. Toss with the olive oil, salt, and add a squeeze of lime juice or vinegar, if you like. Garnish with the sprouts just before serving.

**SERVES 6 AS A FIRST COURSE**

CARLO PETRINI HAS A WORLD LEADER'S FORCE OF personality and a witty, hearty, childlike exuberance. Alice Waters has a whimsical, slightly distracted air that winningly masks a world leader's force of will. They know this about each other. The two have become fast friends and allies, and communicate over long dinners not just in the French that is their common language but also with the wordless language common to stars everywhere.

Alice, as the world calls her, made finding ingredients from local farmers and fishermen essential for any restaurant that cares about the food and the customers it serves, and the environment they all live in. It was only natural that she become the face of Slow Food in the United States. Her early and full embrace of the organization brought it credibility—and, crucially, members—when the national office opened in 2000. Her uncompromising and relentless quest for purity has defined Slow Food USA and brought a new dimension to the international Slow Food movement.

Chez Panisse, the restaurant she founded in 1971, has launched dozens of restaurants across the country whose owners and cooks look to local farms for their supplies. Waters now concentrates on bringing gardens to public schools, allowing children to learn with happily dirty hands the connection between farm and table. "De-*li*-cious" food, as Alice would say, is the eternal link.

# SOFT-SHELL CRAB BISQUE

*As the years have gone by, the food at Chez Panisse, first rooted in Alice Waters's beloved Provence, has only become more direct and true to the ingredients at its heart. A case in point is this soup, sweetened with corn and gentle, low-acid yellow tomato. It comes into its glory with soft-shell crabs sautéed in a light dusting of corn flour. You'll need only a very shallow pool of bisque under the crab—the flavor is intense.*

❋ ❋ ❋ ❋ ❋ ❋ ❋ ❋

**BISQUE:**
2 tablespoons unsalted butter
1 small yellow onion, thinly
    sliced
1 leek (white part only), thinly
    sliced
1 small clove garlic, sliced
½ teaspoon minced fresh thyme
1 yellow tomato, peeled and
    diced

2½ cups water
Salt to taste
3 tablespoons olive oil
1 soft-shell crab, gills removed
1 cup fresh corn kernels (about
    2 large ears)
Freshly ground black pepper,
    cayenne pepper, and fresh
    lemon juice to taste

**SOFT-SHELL CRABS:**
¼ cup corn flour
¼ cup all-purpose flour
½ teaspoon salt
Pinch of cayenne pepper
Freshly ground black pepper
    to taste
4 soft-shell crabs
¼ cup olive oil
Chopped fresh green basil and
    purple basil, for garnish

❋ ❋ ❋ ❋ ❋ ❋ ❋ ❋

TO MAKE THE BISQUE: Melt the butter in a medium saucepan over low heat. Add the onion and leek, and gently stew until the onion is translucent, about 3 minutes. Add the garlic, thyme, tomato, water, and a generous pinch of salt, and bring to a simmer.

In the meantime, heat the olive oil in a small sauté pan or skillet over medium heat and add the soft-shell crab. Fry the crab for 2 to 3 minutes on each side. Add the crab to the soup along with the corn kernels and simmer for 10 minutes. Pour the soup into a blender and purée until smooth. Taste and adjust the seasoning with salt, black pepper, cayenne, and lemon juice.

TO PREPARE THE CRABS: In a small bowl, combine the flours, salt, cayenne, and black pepper. Stir to blend. Dredge each crab in the flour mixture, making sure to coat the entire surface. Heat the olive oil in a large skillet over medium high-heat and fry the crabs for 2 to 3 minutes on each side. Using tongs, transfer to paper towels to drain.

To serve, ladle about ¾ cup of the bisque into each warmed soup bowl and float 1 crab on top. Garnish with the basil.

**SERVES 4 AS A FIRST COURSE**

# Monterey Bay Sardine Toasts with Garden Lettuces

*These are designed around perfectly fresh sardines. That's part of what makes Chez Panisse food so celebrated—absolute reliance on freshness and quality. But don't despair. You can substitute fresh mackerel or anchovies, or any other strong "blue" fish in this recipe. This is the sort of dish Chez Panisse popularized in much of America: a few very good ingredients magically transformed by quick heat.*

❊ ❊ ❊ ❊ ❊ ❊ ❊ ❊ ❊

6 very fresh sardines
2 cloves garlic, sliced thin
½ lemon, thinly sliced, plus
    juice of ½ lemon
Several chervil, summer or
    winter savory, parsley, and
    thyme sprigs

4 bay leaves
Pinch of Maras pepper (Turkish
    red pepper flakes) or red
    pepper flakes
2 to 3 tablespoons extra-virgin
    olive oil, plus more for
    drizzling

Twelve ½-inch-thick slices
    sweet baguette
Salt and freshly ground black
    pepper to taste
3 handfuls young salad greens

❊ ❊ ❊ ❊ ❊ ❊ ❊ ❊ ❊

Fillet the sardines and put them in a shallow dish. Evenly distribute the garlic, lemon slices, fresh herbs, bay leaves, and red pepper flakes over the sardines. Pour 2 to 3 tablespoons olive oil on top. Cover and refrigerate for at least 1 hour or up to 4 hours.

Preheat the oven to 450°F. Place 1 sardine on each slice of baguette, with the silvery skin facing up. Season with salt and black pepper,

and drizzle a little of the marinade on top. Place the toasts on a baking sheet and bake in the oven until heated through, 4 to 5 minutes.

Meanwhile, gently toss the salad greens with the lemon juice, a drizzle of olive oil, and salt and black pepper. Serve the sardine toasts warm, with the salad greens on the side.

**SERVES 6 AS A FIRST COURSE**

# WILD MUSHROOM PASTA HANDKERCHIEFS

*This Chez Panisse legend, a glorious assembly of tissue-thin leaves of pasta layered with a deep-flavored sauté of mushrooms and then crisped in the oven, was adapted from the* Chez Panisse Café Cookbook *(HarperCollins). It's an all-day project to make with friends and serve to more friends—the next day or even the day after that, as all the components can be made in advance.*

❋ ❋ ❋ ❋ ❋ ❋ ❋ ❋

8 ounces mixed wild mushrooms, such as chanterelles, porcini, hedgehogs, and black trumpets
2 tablespoons unsalted butter, plus 2 tablespoons melted unsalted butter

Salt and freshly ground black pepper to taste
1 onion, finely diced
1 teaspoon minced fresh thyme
3 cloves garlic, minced
½ cup crème fraîche
½ cup chicken stock

Pasta Dough (recipe follows)
½ cup grated Parmigiano-Reggiano cheese
4 handfuls curly cress
Lemon juice to taste
Extra-virgin olive oil, for drizzling

❋ ❋ ❋ ❋ ❋ ❋ ❋ ❋

Carefully clean the mushrooms by brushing them or, if they are very dirty, quickly swish them in warm water, then immediately drain and blot dry. Trim the ends and chop the mushrooms into coarse quarters and slices.

Melt 1 tablespoon of the butter in a heavy sauce pan over medium heat. Add the mushrooms, salt and black pepper, and sauté for up to 6 minutes, or until tender. Transfer to a bowl and set aside.

In the same pan, melt the remaining 1 tablespoon butter over medium heat and sauté the onion until translucent, about 4 minutes. Add the thyme, garlic, salt to taste, and cooked mushrooms. Reduce the heat and cook for 5 minutes. Stir in the crème fraîche and chicken stock. Simmer for 3 minutes, or until slightly reduced but still quite juicy. Taste and adjust the seasoning, if necessary.

Preheat the oven to 500°F. Cut the pasta into eight 4½-inch squares. Cook a few squares at a time in a large amount of salted boiling water until barely al dente, 1 to 2 minutes. Transfer to a cold-water bath for a few seconds, then drain and lay the squares flat in one layer on a clean cloth.

Butter four 6-inch earthenware baking dishes. Put 2 cooked pasta squares side by side in the bottom of each dish, overlapping them slightly at the center so the pasta edges hang over the sides. Divide the mushroom sauce among the 4 dishes. Fold the pasta edges loosely back toward the center over the sauce, leaving a wrinkled, dimpled surface. Brush with the melted butter and sprinkle with the grated cheese. Bake until the edges and peaks of the pasta are crisp, 6 to 8 minutes.

Meanwhile, lightly dress the curly cress with salt, a few drops of lemon juice, and a drizzle of olive oil. Carefully slip the pasta out of the baking dishes onto 4 plates; pour any remaining juice over the top. Tuck the curly cress around each portion.

**SERVES 4 AS A FIRST COURSE**

**VARIATION:** For a more lavish version, cook ½ cup finely diced celery root with the onion until soft, and add some minced black truffle along with the crème fraîche and chicken stock.

# PASTA DOUGH

2½ cups unbleached all-purpose
    flour
1 teaspoon salt

3 eggs
3 egg yolks
1 tablespoon olive oil

1 tablespoon water, plus extra
    if needed

❊ ❊ ❊ ❊ ❊ ❊ ❊ ❊ ❊

Mix the flour and salt together and place in a mound on a work surface. In a bowl, beat the eggs, egg yolks, olive oil, and the 1 tablespoon water together. Make a well in the center of the flour and pour in the egg mixture. Begin stirring the eggs with a fork, slowly incorporating the flour from the inner rim of the well. When the mixture has thickened, use a dough scraper to scrape the board and combine all of the ingredients. Slowly begin kneading the dough, using a pushing and squeezing motion. (Alternatively, mix the dough in the bowl of a heavy-duty mixer, using the paddle attachment.) The mixture should appear fairly dry and crumbly. If it is too crumbly, add more water, 1 teaspoon at a time. If the dough is slightly sticky, slowly incorporate more flour as you knead. The dough should contain just enough moisture to bind the flour.

Knead the dough until it has absorbed all of the flour and you can form it into a rough ball. It will not yet appear smooth and elastic; additional kneading will be done with the pasta machine. Flatten the dough ball, wrap it tightly in plastic wrap, and let rest for 4 to 5 minutes.

Divide the dough in half. Flatten 1 piece of the dough with a rolling pin and pass it through the rollers of a pasta machine at its widest setting. Sprinkle the resulting sheet of dough lightly with flour and fold it into thirds. Press the dough down with your fingertips and pass it through the rollers again. Repeat the rolling and folding process at the same setting until the dough is very smooth. Wrap the dough tightly in plastic and let rest for 5 to 10 minutes. Repeat with the second piece of dough.

The dough is now ready to be stretched. Adjust the rollers to the next setting and pass the dough through successively narrower settings (it should be very thin), sprinkling it very lightly with flour if necessary. Test for thickness by cooking a piece of pasta in salted boiling water.

**MAKES 1 POUND**

# APRICOT TART

*Alan Tangren, the co-pastry chef at Chez Panisse, follows a long tradition of multiply gifted people who come to the restaurant and simply stay there, going from post to post largely inventing their roles and reinventing the restaurant in the process. Tangren was the original, and longtime, "forager," the person who went from farm to farm to find heirloom beets and plump quail and greengage plums. ✳ His heart, it turned out, was in pastry, and he has been a brilliant successor to the founding pastry chef, Lindsey Shere. This tart drove Tasha Prysi, who tested the recipes for this book, wild with desire when she worked at Chez Panisse. "When it was on the menu not a shift went by that I didn't sneak a piece," she says. The combination of caramelized crust, juice-absorbing frangipane, and ripe fruit makes this a perfect example of its form, and of the modest genius that continues to make Chez Panisse a national inspiration.*

✳ ✳ ✳ ✳ ✳ ✳ ✳ ✳ ✳

Tart Dough (recipe follows)
¼ cup Frangipane at room temperature (recipe follows)
2 tablespoons flour
3 tablespoons plus ¼ cup sugar

2 tablespoons almonds, ground (optional)
1½ pounds firm, ripe apricots, quartered and pitted
2 tablespoons unsalted butter, melted

½ cup apricot jam, forced through a sieve
Whipped cream or ice cream for serving

✳ ✳ ✳ ✳ ✳ ✳ ✳ ✳ ✳

On a lightly floured surface, roll the dough out into a 14-inch round about ⅛ inch thick. Brush off the excess flour and transfer the dough to a parchment-lined baking sheet. Refrigerate for at least 30 minutes or up to 24 hours.

Preheat the oven to 400°F. If you have a baking stone, place it on a rack in the lower third of the oven.

Remove the dough round from the refrigerator. Spread the frangipane on the dough in an even layer, leaving a 1½-inch border. Mix the flour with 1 tablespoon of the sugar and the ground almonds, if you like, and sprinkle the mixture over the frangipane.

Arrange the apricots in concentric circles on the dough, cut-side up, leaving the 1½-inch border bare. Tilt the ends slightly upwards, so they will caramelize nicely in the oven. Sprinkle the ¼ cup sugar over the fruit.

Rotating the tart, fold the border of exposed dough over itself at regular intervals, crimping and pushing it up against the outer circle of fruit to make a containing rim that resembles a length of rope. Pinch off any excess dough. This rim will contain the juices while the tart is cooking, so check carefully for any low spots and try to build them up. Brush the rim lightly but thoroughly with the melted butter and sprinkle with the remaining 2 tablespoons sugar.

Bake in the lower third of the oven, rotating the pan every 20 minutes or so to ensure even baking. The tart will be done after 45 to 55 minutes. The edges should be dark brown and caramelized, and the tips of some of the fruit should be nearly black. Remove from the oven and let cool for several minutes, then slide the tart off the parchment directly onto a wire rack. Let cool for at least 20 minutes before serving. The tart is best eaten within a few hours of baking.

To serve, warm the apricot jam and brush it gently onto the fruit. Serve with whipped cream or ice cream.

**SERVES 8 TO 10**

## TART DOUGH

1 cup all-purpose flour
½ teaspoon sugar
⅛ teaspoon salt

6 tablespoons cold unsalted butter, cut into ½-inch pieces

¼ cup ice water

❊ ❊ ❊ ❊ ❊ ❊ ❊ ❊

Combine the flour, sugar, and salt in a large bowl. Add the butter and squeeze and break up the pieces with your fingertips until the largest pieces of butter are the size of large lima beans.

Toss the flour mixture with one hand while dribbling in half of the water. Break up the largest pieces of butter while mixing and tossing. Continue to add water until the dough mostly clings together and there are only a few dry particles in the bottom of the bowl. Press the dough into a ball and wrap tightly in plastic wrap, pressing down to flatten it into a disk. Refrigerate for at least 1 hour or up to 24 hours. (The dough can also be frozen at this point for up to 2 weeks.)

**MAKES ENOUGH FOR 1 TART**

## FRANGIPANE

⅓ cup (3 ounces) almond paste
2 teaspoons sugar

2 tablespoons unsalted butter at room temperature
1 tablespoon flour

1 egg
Pinch of salt

❊ ❊ ❊ ❊ ❊ ❊ ❊ ❊

In a medium bowl, blend the almond paste and sugar with a wooden spoon. Beat in the butter. Mix in the flour, egg, and salt, and beat until completely blended. Use immediately, or cover and refrigerate for up to 1 week.

**MAKES ½ CUP**

JUDY RODGERS
*Zuni Café*
*San Francisco*
**CALIFORNIA**

JUDY RODGERS IS ONE OF SEVERAL PRODIGIOUSLY talented Chez Panisse alumni who have continued to set national trends on their own. Her Zuni Café, a marvelous warren of high-ceilinged rooms on Market Street, in San Francisco, is always perfumed with her signature wood-roasted chicken, and animated by diners who know they'll get good, honest food.

Rodgers has spent a lot of time in Italy savoring country dishes. The quality that makes her food different from that of so many cooks who have fallen under Italy's spell is that she knows how to make it practical in American restaurant kitchens. The simplicity and rightness of Italian food suit the perfectly fresh ingredients she can find, and ease the continental transition. Rodgers also has the gift of transmitting the spirit of her food to a home kitchen.

# ZUNI HOUSE-CURED ANCHOVIES

*The first course for any Zuni regular are these home-cured anchovies. With their plush texture, flavor that is not too fishy or salty, and glinting titanium-bright skin, they come as a revelation to the typical anchovy hater. Be sure to serve them with crisp, palate-cleansing celery and lemon wedges, along with olives and radishes. You can serve the anchovies within a day of their second salting, although they will keep for months in salt.*

❊ ❊ ❊ ❊ ❊ ❊ ❊ ❊ ❊

1 pound fresh whole anchovies (16 to 20 fish)
2 pounds rock salt

About 1 cup extra-virgin olive oil

Lemon wedges and black olives, radishes, and/or slivered celery for serving

❊ ❊ ❊ ❊ ❊ ❊ ❊ ❊ ❊

Rinse the anchovies under a gentle stream of cold water. Pinch off the heads; the entrails should come out with them. Slide a finger into each body cavity, gently prying it open as you go. Briefly rinse each fish again, this time targeting the inside of the body. Spread on paper towels to drain. Place the anchovies in a colander over a plate or bowl, sprinkling each layer with rock salt as you go and using about 1 cup total of the salt. Cover loosely with plastic wrap and refrigerate for 8 to 12 hours.

Remove the anchovies from the salt; they will be slightly stiffer. Place in a wide-mouth jar, carefully layering with the remaining 1½ cups salt. Cover tightly and refrigerate for at least 1 hour or up to 2 weeks.

To serve, remove the fish from the salt. They will be quite firm. One by one, rinse them under cold running water, rubbing to remove the scales. The fish will soften somewhat as you do this. Starting at the belly or near the dorsal fin, use your fingers to gently peel the fillets off the backbone. If a fillet starts to tear, the fish may still be too dry; soak it briefly in water to further soften the flesh, then try again. Once you have filleted all the fish, use a paring knife to trim off the fins and ragged edges and to scrape off any remaining scales. The fillets should be mildly salty and fairly soft; if still hard or very salty, soak in cold water until tender and tasty. Arrange the fillets on a towel, cover with a second towel, and press hard to draw out as much water as possible. Lift the top towel, replace it in a slightly different position, and press again to draw out even more water. Place the fillets in a small bowl and add extra-virgin olive oil to cover. Garnish serving plate with lemon wedges, black olives, whole or sliced radishes, and slivered celery.

**SERVES 4 TO 6 AS A FIRST COURSE**

# LAMB CHOPS AND GRILLED ZUCCHINI WITH VINEGAR AND MINT

*Judy Rodgers took the idea for the zucchini, grilled and strewn with mint leaves and bathed in sweetened vinegar, from a typical Sicilian dish. It's one of the best ways to cook zucchini, alone or as a side dish, and perfectly complements grilled lamb chops. This is an ideal example of California cuisine: not precious or trendy but instead simple, direct, and reliant on good raw materials.*

❊ ❊ ❊ ❊ ❊ ❊ ❊ ❊ ❊

4 to 6 lamb chops
Salt and freshly ground black
   pepper to taste

**GRILLED ZUCCHINI:**
1 pound zucchini
Salt to taste
2 teaspoons mild olive oil
12 fresh mint leaves

1 tablespoon champagne vinegar
2 teaspoons sugar
Freshly ground black pepper
   to taste
Extra-virgin olive oil for
   drizzling

❊ ❊ ❊ ❊ ❊ ❊ ❊ ❊ ❊

Season the lamb chops with salt and black pepper. Set aside. Cut the zucchini into ⅓-inch-thick lengthwise slices. Sprinkle lightly and evenly with salt. Set aside on paper towels.

Light a fire in a charcoal grill and let it burn to glowing red coals. Grill the lamb chops for 4 to 5 minutes on each side for medium-rare. Transfer the chops to a warm place on one side of the grill. Pat the zucchini dry, then coat with the mild olive oil. Arrange in a single layer on the grill. Cook until tender and grilled-marked, 1 to 2 minutes on each side.

While the zucchini are grilling, coarsely chop the mint leaves and stir together the vinegar and sugar.

Remove the zucchini from the grill and arrange in a shallow baking dish. Scatter the mint over the zucchini, then drizzle with the sweetened vinegar. Add a few grinds of black pepper and drizzle with the extra-virgin olive oil. Tilt the dish to distribute the seasonings. Serve the lamb chops on warmed plates with the zucchini alongside.

**SERVES 4 TO 6 AS A MAIN COURSE**

# Arugula Salad with Baked Ricotta and Cherry Tomatoes

*Here is another dish that depends on the freshness of its ingredients, particularly sweet cherry tomatoes and, ideally, the divine sheep's milk ricotta. Baking any ricotta gives it mellow interest and an easily spreadable consistency. This can go over toast or right over the peppery dressed greens.*

❄ ❄ ❄ ❄ ❄ ❄ ❄ ❄ ❄

1½ cups (12 ounces) fresh
    ricotta cheese, preferably
    sheep's milk ricotta
Salt to taste
1 small clove garlic, halved

4 small handfuls arugula leaves,
    or 1 bunch arugula, stemmed
2 tablespoons extra-virgin
    olive oil
About 1 tablespoon red wine
    vinegar or sherry vinegar

About 24 Sweet 100 or Sungold
    cherry tomatoes, stemmed
    and halved
Freshly ground black pepper
    to taste

❄ ❄ ❄ ❄ ❄ ❄ ❄ ❄ ❄

Preheat the broiler. Put the ricotta in a small bowl and beat with a wooden spoon to soften. Season with salt. Place in a shallow 1-cup gratin dish and spread to make a fairly even layer; don't bother to smooth the surface, as little crags of cheese will bake darker than the rest and provide flavor and texture. Place under the broiler 6 inches from the heating element and bake until heated through, 10 to 15 minutes. The surface should be speckled with dark brown to black char marks. Remove from the broiler and set aside.

Rub the cut garlic over the inside of a large salad bowl. Add the arugula and a few pinches of salt. Gently toss the arugula with the olive oil. Add the vinegar and toss again. Taste and adjust the seasoning, if necessary. Add the tomatoes and fold gently to distribute. Arrange the salad on individual plates. Garnish each plate with a few wedges of the warm cheese and freshly ground black pepper.

**SERVES 4 AS A FIRST COURSE**

# BLACKBERRY PEACH SUMMER PUDDING

*Summer pudding is dessert perfection, at once distilling and ennobling its ingredients. Judy Rodgers's version of a proud part of British heritage uses only blackberries and peaches, but for a more British experience you can substitute raspberries or mixed berries and currants. The rose geranium–scented (or plain vanilla) crème anglaise is another English inspiration. The light, yolky sauce is so good with the sweet-tart pudding that you should make it even if no rose geraniums fill your garden pots.*

❈ ❈ ❈ ❈ ❈ ❈ ❈ ❈ ❈

3 cups fresh blackberries
¼ cup sugar
1 peach
1½ teaspoons dry white
    vermouth

Twelve ⅛-inch-thick slices
    white sandwich bread,
    crusts trimmed
Rose Geranium Custard Sauce
    (recipe follows)

❈ ❈ ❈ ❈ ❈ ❈ ❈ ❈ ❈

Sort through the berries and discard any that have even a speck of mold. Put the sugar and 1 cup of the berries in a medium sauté pan or skillet and cook over medium heat just until the sugar dissolves and the berries release their juice. Remove from the heat and smash a few of the berries to release more juice. Fold in the remaining berries. Set aside.

Immerse the peach in a saucepan of gently simmering water for 10 to 20 seconds, or until the skin loosens from the flesh. Transfer to a bowl of ice water for 1 minute or so. Drain, remove the skin, and trim any bruises. Cut the peach in half, remove the pit, and cut the fruit into ¼-inch dice. You should have about ⅔ cup. Add the vermouth and diced peach to the berries, then fold to combine. Mash additional berries, one or two at a time, until the liquid reaches one-fourth of the depth of the fruit.

Cut 8 slices of the bread into 8 rounds sized to fit the bottom and top of four 6-ounce ramekins. Cut the remaining 4 slices bread into long strips sized to fit around the sides of the ramekins.

Line the bottom and sides of the ramekins with the cut bread. Stir the berry mixture well and divide it among the 4 ramekins, making sure to distribute both the fruit and juice equally. Top the cups with the remaining bread rounds and press down. The cups should be brimming full. Put the cups on a baking sheet and cover with a sheet of plastic wrap or parchment paper. Put a second baking sheet on top and top with a weight. Let sit for 3 to 4 hours to let the bread absorb the juice.

To serve the puddings, slide a knife around the edge of each mold. Place a dessert plate upside down on the top of each pudding. Hold the ramekin in place and invert the pudding onto the plate. Tap the ramekin to encourage the pudding to come out, then gently lift. If the circle of bread sticks to the bottom, remove it with the tip of a paring knife or small fork and replace it on top of the pudding. Spoon the custard sauce around the puddings and serve.

**SERVES 4**

## ROSE GERANIUM CUSTARD SAUCE

3 egg yolks
2 tablespoons sugar

¾ cup heavy cream
1 large or 2 or 3 small rose
    geranium leaves

Pinch of salt
3 tablespoons whole milk

✥ ✥ ✥ ✥ ✥ ✥ ✥ ✥ ✥

In a small bowl, whisk the egg yolks and sugar together. Gradually whisk in the cream. Add the geranium leaves and salt, and pour into a small, heavy saucepan. Cook over low heat, stirring constantly, taking care to scrape the sides and bottom of the pan, until the mixture is thick and satiny, 8 to 10 minutes. Remove from the heat. Stir in the milk and immediately pour the mixture through a fine-mesh sieve into a bowl. Retrieve the geranium leaves from the sieve and replace in the hot custard. Let cool, stirring occasionally, crushing the leaves against the side of the bowl to release their flavor. Cover and refrigerate for at least 1 hour or up to 5 days.

**MAKES ABOUT 1 CUP**

PAUL BERTOLLI WAS ONE OF THE MOST INFLUENTIAL chefs at Chez Panisse, and is the author, with Alice Waters, of a true kitchen classic, *Chez Panisse Cooking* (Random House). His approach to food is both scholarly and scientific, and immensely respectful. He may not have the national profile that Waters does, but in the Bay Area, Bertolli is something of a god. The reasons are similar: he comes to know food intimately, and that intimate knowledge and respect are clear in the food he serves at Oliveto, a restaurant just a few miles from Chez Panisse.

Bertolli is now obtaining humanely raised animals and butchering them himself to create a series of home-cured products of the kind every country farm in Italy, southern France, and Spain used to make as a matter of course. His own map has come chiefly from Italy, where Bertolli has toured butchering and meat shops and befriended artisans who might be the last sources for techniques on how to make *soppressata* or salami or prosciutto.

Curing meat is slow. Bertolli spends more and more time in his butchering workshop, mixing, tying, and hanging meats to cure for weeks and months. He is also trying to defy centuries of hallowed Italian tradition in his aging loft in the Bay Area wine country, where he makes his own "Agro Dolce" balsamic vinegar—a process that takes decades, not months. It's Bertolli's way of saying that America can have Slow traditions, too, ones that grandchildren can enjoy and pass on to the next generation.

# CARPACCIO OF VEAL WITH OLD BALSAMICO

*Paul Bertolli's attention to humanely raised animals gave rise to this carpaccio of pounded raw veal seasoned simply and, like so much of what his fellow Chez Panisse alumni create, dependent on perfect ingredients for its quality. Bertolli's own secret ingredient is his lovingly and laboriously aged balsamic vinegar, but this recipe will showcase any fine balsamic.*

❄ ❄ ❄ ❄ ❄ ❄ ❄ ❄

¼ cup pure olive oil
12 thin slices (12 ounces) veal scallopine, membrane free

3 teaspoons extra-virgin olive oil
1½ teaspoons sea salt
Freshly ground black pepper to taste

4-ounce chunk of Parmigiano-Reggiano cheese
Aged balsamic vinegar, for drizzling

❄ ❄ ❄ ❄ ❄ ❄ ❄ ❄

Cut twelve 6-inch squares of parchment paper. Brush a piece of paper with some of the pure olive oil and place 2 slices of the veal in the center. Brush the veal with pure olive oil and cover with another piece of parchment paper. Using a flat-sided meat mallet, gently pound the veal to a ¹⁄₁₆-inch thickness; repeat this process with the remaining veal. Cover and refrigerate for at least 1 hour or up to 4 hours.

To serve, remove the top layer of parchment and invert the veal onto a chilled salad plate. Press down gently on the veal, making sure that all of it is touching the plate, then remove the other layer of parchment. To finish, drizzle each serving of carpaccio with ½ teaspoon of the extra-virgin olive oil and lightly spread it over the meat. Next, sprinkle each serving with ¼ teaspoon sea salt and a twist or two of freshly ground black pepper. Finally, shave Parmigiano-Reggiano cheese over the carpaccio and drizzle the balsamic over each portion.

**SERVES 6 AS A FIRST COURSE**

# Spelt Tagliatelle with Duck Giblets

*This is one of the most old-fashioned, "authentic" dishes imaginable—the sort of cooking born of need and availability that Slow Food celebrates and wants to preserve. Spelt, an ancient wheat variety that fed Roman armies, has come back into fashion, valued today not just for its nutty flavor but also for its ability to be tolerated by those allergic to gluten. (You can substitute whole-wheat pastry flour, but the pasta will break in the mouth rather than being pliant and yielding.) Spelt's heartiness makes it stand up to the strong flavors of giblets, which anyone who has ever loved a good homemade gravy of velvety French chicken sauce will recognize and appreciate.*

❊ ❊ ❊ ❊ ❊ ❊ ❊ ❊ ❊

**PASTA DOUGH:**
2 cups spelt flour
2 eggs
Water, if needed

2 pounds duck hearts and
    gizzards
2 tablespoons olive oil
Sea salt and freshly ground
    black pepper to taste
1 large carrot, peeled and
    finely diced

½ stalk celery, finely diced
1 small yellow onion, finely
    diced
3⅓ cups duck or chicken stock
5 tablespoons unsalted butter
Grated Parmigiano-Reggiano
    cheese, for serving

❊ ❊ ❊ ❊ ❊ ❊ ❊ ❊ ❊

TO MAKE THE PASTA DOUGH: In a large bowl, combine the flour and eggs. Mix with a fork and then, on a floured surface, begin to knead the dough with your hands. If the dough feels dry, add a few teaspoons of water and knead until it gathers into a ball. Continue kneading until the dough feels springy. Wrap the dough in plastic wrap and let stand for 1 hour.

MEANWHILE, MAKE THE SAUCE: Cut the duck hearts in half. Position the gizzards so that the rounded lobes are facing up and the connective membrane is on the cutting board. Cut the red lobes away from the bluish-white skin to which they are attached. Heat the olive oil in a heavy, 3-quart soup pot or Dutch oven over medium heat. Add the gizzards and hearts, season with salt and black pepper, and increase the heat to medium-high. The hearts and gizzards will release their juices. Cook to reduce the juices, 5 to 8 minutes. Reduce the

heat to medium and cook the giblets, stirring often, until they are browned all over, about 20 minutes.

Add the vegetables and cook another 10 minutes. Add ½ cup of the stock and stir to scrape up the browned bits on the bottom of the pot. Add 2½ cups more stock, bring to a simmer, and cook for 1 hour, or until the stock has nearly evaporated and the gizzards are tender. If they are not, add a ladle or two of water and continue to cook until done.

Turn the gizzards and hearts out onto a cutting board and chop them finely. Set aside in a bowl.

Divide the dough in half. Flatten one piece of the dough with a rolling pin and pass it through the roller of a pasta machine at its widest setting. Sprinkle the sheet of dough lightly with flour and fold it into thirds. Press the dough down with your fingertips and pass it through the roller again. Repeat the process, ending by using the No. 5 setting. Repeat with the second piece of dough. Cut the sheets into 8-inch lengths and flour them on both sides. Roll up each piece of pasta and cut it into tagliatelle (about ¼ inch wide).

Transfer the giblets to a medium saucepan, add the remaining ⅓ cup stock, and bring to a simmer over medium heat. Stir in the butter,

then cook the sauce until slightly thickened, 3 to 4 minutes. Taste and adjust the seasoning, if necessary.

In a large pot of salted boiling water, cook the noodles until al dente, 2 to 3 minutes. Drain and toss with the hot sauce. Serve with the cheese alongside.

**SERVES 8 AS A MAIN COURSE**

# TRAMEZZINO OF SAND DABS WITH TWO TOMATO SAUCES

*Two populations seem able to coax magic from seemingly simple sets of ingredients and a limited range of cooking techniques: Italians and northern Californians. Paul Bertolli uses two colors of tomatoes and almost nothing else to make this perfect fish dish. He recommends sand dabs or sole, but any small, fresh white fish will be more than well served.*

❄ ❄ ❄ ❄ ❄ ❄ ❄ ❄

**TOMATO SAUCE:**
8 ounces red tomatoes, chopped
8 ounces yellow tomatoes, chopped
Sea salt to taste

2 tablespoons unsalted butter
2 leeks (white part only), finely chopped
Sea salt to taste
¼ cup water
3 tablespoons minced fresh flat-leaf parsley

6 unskinned sand dabs or petrale sole, filleted, dorsal bones trimmed away
6 tablespoons extra-virgin olive oil

❄ ❄ ❄ ❄ ❄ ❄ ❄ ❄

TO MAKE THE SAUCES: Heat a 9½-inch sauté pan or skillet over medium heat. Add the red tomatoes and increase the heat to high. Cook the tomatoes until just soft, 2 to 3 minutes. Transfer to a bowl. Repeat the process with the yellow tomatoes. Pass each bowl of tomatoes through the fine-mesh blade of a food mill into separate bowls. Season the sauces with sea salt and set aside.

Melt the butter in a small sauté pan or skillet over low heat. Add the leeks, a pinch of salt, and the water. Cover and cook the leeks until meltingly soft, 8 to 10 minutes. Remove from heat and let cool. Add the parsley.

Lightly salt the fillets on both sides and place on a work surface, skin-side down, in pairs,

matching left and right filleted sides. Spread a thin layer of the leek mixture on each of the left-side fillets and top it symmetrically with the matching right-side fillet to form a sandwich.

Heat 2 tablespoons of the olive oil in a large seasoned or nonstick skillet over medium-high heat. Place the fish stacks in the pan and brown thoroughly on each side, 5 to 7 minutes total. Take care when turning the stacks not to break or separate them.

Transfer a stack to each of 6 warmed plates. Reheat the sauces separately and stir 2 tablespoons extra-virgin olive oil into each. Spoon a little of each tomato sauce around each stack and serve immediately.

**SERVES 6 AS A FIRST COURSE**

**JUNE TAYLOR**
*Oakland*
**CALIFORNIA**

JUNE TAYLOR WANTS TO REFRESH AND REINVIGORATE a hallowed British tradition on American soil: making marmalade and fruit conserves. She happens to live and work in the ideal place—the food paradise of the Bay Area, where fresh fruit of the kind she grew up eating near London is available for much of the year, and where people who appreciate good and genuine food will support her painstaking and original work.

Putting up fruit at home used to be the regular habit of anyone who lived near an orchard. The custom died out as freezing and refrigeration became common and time became short. Americans relied on industrial producers after World War II, and so did Britons, who were and remain particularly passionate about marmalade and jam.

Taylor grew up in a countrified London suburb in the 1950s with a strong love of making things by hand: she actually enjoyed home economics and took seven years of it before deciding to study sociology and work in education. But she grew weary of the academic life, and followed a traveling whim to California, where she met the man she decided to marry.

Her lifelong love of craft and aesthetics led Taylor, who is a plain-spoken, eloquent, and engaging woman, first to baking bread, an activity much in vogue in northern California. Eventually she turned to fruit and her country's traditions. Love of craft keeps Taylor contentedly bent over steaming pots, and peeling and cutting pounds and pounds of plums, apricots, oranges, and pears.

And then there is the pursuit of the fruit. Finding sources for the best fruit led to a deep conviction that only organic fruit would do. That's what she wants to feed her family and the customers who throng her booth at the San Francisco Ferry Plaza Saturday farmers' market, where Taylor beams as people spoon out samples of her jewel-like jams and marmalades.

# APRICOTS IN ALMOND SYRUP

*Love of the beauty of fresh fruit and the tactile pleasure of sorting through and preparing it were part of June Taylor's reason for making marmalade her business. Here is a good introduction to home canning, a way of holding on to the evanescent apricot season in early summer and feeling the tactile pleasure for yourself. Use firm, almost-ripe apricots; as with all her recipes, Taylor specifies only organically raised fruit.*

✳ ✳ ✳ ✳ ✳ ✳ ✳ ✳ ✳

12 cups sugar
8 cups water
½ cup fresh lemon juice

Strips from 2 orange peels
4 pounds firm, ripe apricots, preferably organic, halved and pitted

1¼ teaspoons almond extract

✳ ✳ ✳ ✳ ✳ ✳ ✳ ✳ ✳

Preheat the oven to 250°F.

In a large, heavy pot, combine the sugar and water. Stir to dissolve. Add the lemon juice and orange peels. Bring the mixture to a boil over medium-high heat and boil for 10 minutes. Remove the orange peels.

Meanwhile, put 5 or 6 one-pound (16-ounce) wide-mouth canning jars in the oven to heat or place the jars in a large stockpot filled with water. Bring the water to a low boil and leave the jars for 15 minutes. Turn off the heat, leaving the jars in the hot water. Put the apricots in the simmering syrup and cover with a round of parchment paper to keep the fruit submerged. Reduce the heat to medium-low and remove the paper to stir frequently until the mixture simmers again. Test the fruit immediately; at this point, the apricots should be tender when pierced, but still hold their shape. If not, simmer a few more minutes. Be careful not to overcook the apricots.

While the apricots are cooking, carefully remove 1 cup of the poaching syrup and stir in the almond extract. Working quickly, with one jar at a time, put about 1 tablespoon of the almond-flavored syrup in the bottom of the hot jar and carefully pack the jar half full with apricots. Add almond syrup until it reaches the level of the apricots. Continue packing the jar with apricots until full. Add more of the almond syrup until it covers the apricots and is within ⅛ inch of the rim. Repeat for each jar, flavoring and adding more syrup as needed.

Screw the lids on tightly and leave, undisturbed, until a vacuum seal has been achieved, at least 2 hours. Store in the cupboard for up to 1 year. Once opened, store in the refrigerator for no more than 6 months.

**MAKES 5 OR 6 SIXTEEN-OUNCE JARS**

# SANTA ROSA PLUM CONSERVE

*This seemingly simple recipe is actually the imparting of a near-lifetime of judicious experience in how to get the most flavor from Santa Rosa plums, a matchless summer fruit with a balance of sweetness and acidity that makes them seem lightly spicy and never cloying. June Taylor macerates the fruit flesh in sugar and lemon juice before boiling it just long enough to turn it into a thick, full-flavored sauce. Like all of Taylor's conserves, this isn't overly sweet, and should be refrigerated after being opened.*

❋ ❋ ❋ ❋ ❋ ❋ ❋ ❋

6 pounds Santa Rosa plums, preferably organic, halved and pitted

2 pounds sugar
⅓ cup fresh lemon juice

❋ ❋ ❋ ❋ ❋ ❋ ❋ ❋

Cut the plums into bite-sized pieces. In a large bowl, alternate layers of plums, sugar, and lemon juice. Cover and refrigerate overnight.

In a large, heavy pot, bring the fruit mixture to a boil and cook, stirring frequently, to a very thick sauce, 25 to 30 minutes.

Meanwhile, place 9 half-pint (8-ounce) canning jars in a large stockpot filled with water. Bring the water to a low boil and leave the jars for 15 minutes. Turn off the heat, leaving the jars in the hot water. When the conserve has reached the desired consistency, remove the jars from the water bath and turn them upside down on dish towels to drain.

Skim the surface of the conserve with a metal spoon to remove any scum. Quickly fill the hot jars within ⅛ inch of the rim. Screw on the lids tightly and leave the jars on a wire rack, undisturbed, until a vacuum seal has been achieved, at least 2 hours. Store in the cupboard for up to 1 year. Once opened, store in the refrigerator for no more than 6 months.

**MAKES ABOUT 9 EIGHT-OUNCE JARS**

# THICK-CUT ORANGE MARMALADE

*A June Taylor masterpiece, worthy of her British heritage. Marmalade, she explains, requires a delicate balance of acid, sugar, and pectin, the thickening agent in fruit. Make this thick and chewy marmalade at the beginning of the season, when oranges have lots of acid and natural pectin: sweet oranges, Taylor says, may well lead to thin marmalade. For thickening insurance, add the membranes and seeds from the lemons to the cotton jelly bag mentioned in the recipe.*

❋ ❋ ❋ ❋ ❋ ❋ ❋ ❋

| 10 pounds Navel or Valencia oranges, preferably organic | ¾ cup fresh lemon juice  3½ cups water | 3½ pounds sugar |

❋ ❋ ❋ ❋ ❋ ❋ ❋ ❋

Using a potato peeler, remove the peel from enough oranges to yield 1½ cups. Cut the peel into ½-inch-thick slices. Cut off the peel of the remaining oranges down to the flesh and discard the peel. Working over a bowl to catch the juice and segments, release the orange segments by cutting the flesh away from either side of each of the membranes. Reserve the membranes and seeds as you go.

In a shallow, heavy pot, combine the orange flesh, peel, lemon juice, and water. Put the reserved orange seeds and membranes in a cotton jelly bag or a square of cheesecloth tied with kitchen twine (leave long ends of the twine) and suspend in the pot. Bring the mixture to a boil and cook until the peel is tender, 25 to 30 minutes.

Remove the jelly bag or cheesecloth square and let it cool to the touch. Add the sugar to the marmalade and stir to dissolve. Squeeze the liquid from the jelly bag into the fruit mixture. This liquid contains the natural pectin, so be sure to squeeze out every last drop. Return

the marmalade to a boil and cook until a jelly thermometer registers 222°F, 25 to 35 minutes.

While the marmalade is cooking, place 9 half-pint (8-ounce) jars in a large pot filled with water. Bring the water to a low boil and leave the jars for 15 minutes. Turn off the heat, but leave the jars in the hot water. When the marmalade has reached the jellying stage, remove the jars from the water bath and turn them upside down on towels to drain. Or follow Taylor's method: heat the jars in a 250°F oven until ready to fill. The important steps, she says, are to fill clean, hot jars with hot marmalade and work fast.

Skim the surface of the marmalade with a metal spoon to remove any scum. Quickly fill the hot jars to within ⅛ inch of the rim. Screw the lids on tightly and let sit on a wire rack, undisturbed, until a vacuum seal has been achieved. Store in the cupboard for up to 1 year. Once opened, store in the refrigerator for no more than 6 months.

**MAKES ABOUT 9 HALF-PINT JARS**

ELISABETH PRUEITT IS A MARVELOUSLY TALENTED pastry chef. Together with her husband, Chad Robertson, the attractive couple runs what many people—people like Alice Waters and Paul Bertolli, whose opinions are revered—consider to be the best bakery in the Bay Area. It has the kind of loaf that can inspire cross-country pilgrimages by people already persuaded that the Bay Area has the country's best bread.

Chad Robertson fusses over his sourdough starters and seven kinds of custom-milled flour for his superb, not-too-sour country bread, with its infinitely flavorful crust born of the wood-fired oven he built and lovingly tends. It was Alan Scott, the guru of building wood-fired ovens in America, who first brought the Texas-born Chad to California. Chad had met Elisabeth, who began as an acting student, in a pastry class at the Culinary Institute of America; their names followed each other on the class roster, so they worked at the same wooden board. Dustings of flour led to showerings of rice, though it took a while.

Elisabeth fusses over pastry, experimenting constantly with new techniques and ingredients. She has June Taylor's love of craft and dedication to absolutely fresh, organically raised fruit, and Paul Bertolli's desire to study and surpass European traditions.

# GOUGÈRES

*Here are Elisabeth Prueitt's savory cheese cream puffs, light and simple and an excellent, not-too-filling mouthful to go with predinner drinks.*

❋ ❋ ❋ ❋ ❋ ❋ ❋ ❋ ❋

1¼ cups nonfat milk
⅔ cup (1⅓ sticks) unsalted
 butter
1 teaspoon salt
1 cup bread flour

5 eggs
1 teaspoon freshly ground
 black pepper
1 tablespoon minced fresh herbs,
 such as thyme or chives

1 cup (4 ounces) shredded
 Gruyère cheese
2 egg yolks
1 tablespoon heavy cream

❋ ❋ ❋ ❋ ❋ ❋ ❋ ❋ ❋

Preheat the oven to 350°F. Butter a baking sheet or line it with parchment paper.

In a medium, heavy saucepan, combine the milk, butter, and salt. Cook over medium heat until the butter has melted and the mixture comes to a boil. Add the flour all at once, stirring with a wooden spoon. Stir vigorously until the mixture is a smooth mass and pulls away from the sides of the pan, about 3 minutes.

Add the eggs, one at a time, beating vigorously until each is completely incorporated before adding the next. Fold in the black pepper, herbs, and three-fourths of the cheese.

Scoop out tablespoonfuls of the batter and place them 3 inches apart on the prepared baking sheet.

In a small bowl, whisk the egg yolks and cream together. Brush the egg mixture over each gougère and sprinkle the remaining cheese on top. Bake until puffed and golden brown, 30 to 35 minutes. Serve warm.

**MAKES ABOUT 2 DOZEN PUFFS**

# FRUIT FOCACCIA

*Anyone afraid of yeast bread should try this lightly sweet, buttery sheet-pan bread. It's somewhere between a real bread and a confection, and impossible to keep your hands off, especially when it's warm out of the oven.*

❊ ❊ ❊ ❊ ❊ ❊ ❊ ❊ ❊

⅔ cup (4 ounces) tart dried plums or dried apricots, cut into ½-inch dice
½ cup golden raisins
1¾ cups plus 2 tablespoons water

3 tablespoons honey
¾ teaspoon active dry yeast
1 teaspoon grated orange zest
3¾ cups all-purpose flour
¾ teaspoon salt

7 tablespoons room-temperature unsalted butter, cut up
2 egg yolks
1 tablespoon heavy cream
Coarse sugar for sprinkling

❊ ❊ ❊ ❊ ❊ ❊ ❊ ❊ ❊

Put the plums and raisins in a small bowl, add hot water to cover, and soak for 15 minutes. Drain and let cool.

In the bowl of a heavy-duty mixer fitted with the paddle attachment, combine the water, honey, yeast, and orange zest. Add the flour and salt, and mix on medium speed until smooth. With the machine running, add the butter and mix until blended. Add the fruit and mix again until it is evenly distributed. The dough should be moister and looser than a regular bread dough; add more water if necessary. Cover the bowl with plastic wrap and let rise in a warm place until almost doubled in volume, about 1½ hours.

Butter a 9-by-12-inch baking dish. Transfer the dough to the buttered baking dish. Spread the dough out with moistened fingers, making sure to pull it into the corners of the dish.

In a small bowl, whisk the egg yolks and cream together. Brush the egg mixture on top of the dough and sprinkle with coarse sugar.

Let the dough rise again for 30 to 45 minutes. Meanwhile, preheat the oven to 350°F.

Bake the focaccia until it is golden brown and springs back to the touch, about 30 minutes. Remove from the oven and let cool slightly or completely. Cut into large squares to serve.

**SERVES 8 TO 10**

**NOTE:** After the first rise, the dough may be refrigerated overnight. Allow extra time for the second rise, since the dough will be cold.

# ROCHERS

*Completely addictive, these crisp and crunchy almond meringues are also very easy to make. Once you taste them, you'll want to have a supply on hand at all times, but it's something of a challenge to make enough to last longer than, say, an evening and the next morning.*

❄ ❄ ❄ ❄ ❄ ❄ ❄ ❄ ❄

1 cup (4 ounces) sliced almonds, toasted

2 egg whites
⅔ teaspoon vanilla extract
Pinch of salt

1 cup confectioners' sugar, sifted

❄ ❄ ❄ ❄ ❄ ❄ ❄ ❄ ❄

Preheat the oven to 350°F. In a food processor, pulse the almonds to a coarse grind, or use a rolling pin to break them into ¼-inch pieces. Set aside.

In a large bowl, combine the egg whites, vanilla, and salt. Beat until frothy. Gradually beat in the confectioners' sugar until stiff, glossy peaks form. Fold in the almonds until blended. Immediately put the mixture into a pastry bag fitted with a No. 6 or No. 7 plain round pastry tip. On a baking sheet, pipe out "kisses" about 1¼ inches at the base, with a peak about 2 inches high. Leave a ½-inch space between each cookie. If you don't have a pastry bag, make small rounds by dropping spoonfuls of the meringue onto the baking sheet.

Put the rochers in the oven, leaving the oven door slightly ajar. Bake until slightly puffed but still moist inside, about 15 minutes. If the tops start to brown too much, put a sheet of parchment paper or aluminum foil on top.

**MAKES 28 TO 30 COOKIES**

**NOTE:** Store in an airtight container for up to 1 week. If kept longer, they will dry out completely, but they will still be delicious, and some people prefer them crunchy. To make dry rochers, reduce the oven temperature to 200°F and bake for another 45 minutes.

# SOURCE GUIDE

Here's a list of the artisans and cooks mentioned in this book, along with ways to find their products or ones like them. The list is exceedingly partial, in every sense. These are the people who were extremely generous with their time and knowledge during the writing of this book.

In a few cases the artisans themselves will ship their products. In all cases, cooks and artisans are worth calling or writing. They are usually happy to communicate their love of the land and what they make.

### SLOW FOOD

For more information on Slow Food and an extensive listing of artisans around the world:

www.slowfood.com

International Office
tel: 39 (0)172 419 611
fax: 39 (0)172 421 293
international@slowfood.com
Via della Mendicità Istruita 8
12042 Bra (CN), Italy

Italy
tel: 39 (0)172 419 611
fax: 39 (0)172 421 293
info@slowfood.it

Germany
tel: 49 (0)251 793 368
fax: 49 (0)251 793 366
info@slowfood.de

Switzerland
tel: 41 (0)1 380 3949
fax: 41 (0)1 380 2990
info@slowfood.ch

France
tel: 33 (0)1 455 19044
info@slowfoodfrance.com

USA
tel: 212-965-5640
fax: 212-226-0672
info@slowfoodusa.org

### ARTISANS

#### CHEESE:

Roberto Rubino
Di Gilio Farm
ANFOSC
www.anfosc.it
Viale Basento 108
85100 Potenza, Italy
tel/fax: 36 0971 54661
info@anfosc.it

Cindy and David Major
Vermont Shepherd Cheese
Major Farm
www.vermontshepherd.com
875 Patch Rd.
Putney, VT 05346
tel: 802-387-4473
fax: 802-387-2041
vtshephrd@sover.net

American Cheese Society
www.cheesesociety.org
304 West Liberty St., Ste. 201
Louisville, KY 40202
tel: 502-583-3783
fax: 502-589-3602
acs@hqtrs.com

#### MEAT:

Torsten Kramer
Bio-Fleisherei
Kaninchenbergweg #41
23564 Lübeck, Germany
tel: 49 451 601115
tahsinkramer@aol.com

Verna Dietrich
Dietrich's Meat & Country Store
660 Old 22
Lenhartsville, PA 19534
tel: 610-756-6344

#### SALT:

João Navalho
Necton
www.necton.pt
Belamandil
8700-152 Olhão, Portugal
tel: 351 289703961
info@necton.pt

#### SHELLFISH:

Moore's Stone Crab Restaurant
www.stonecrabstoyourdoor.com
P.O. Box 219
Longboat Key, FL 34228
tel: 941-383-7796
toll-free fax: 1-888-419-CLAW
(2529)

#### WINE:

Inniskillin Wines, Inc.
www.inniskillin.com
1499 Line 3, RR #1
Niagara Parkway
Niagara-on-the-Lake, Ontario,
Canada L0S1J0
tel: 905-468-2187
toll-free: 888-466-4754
fax: 905-468-5355
inniskil@inniskillin.com

André Dubosc
Plaimont
www.plaimont.com
Route d'Orthez
32400 Saint-Mont, France
tel: 33 05 62696287
fax: 33 05 62696168

#### FRUIT:

Stephen Wood
Poverty Lane Orchards
www.povertylaneorchards.com
Farnum Hill Ciders
www.farnumhillciders.com
98 Poverty Ln.
Lebanon, NH 03766
tel: 603-448-1511
fax: 603-448-7326
info@farnumhillciders.com

**VEGETABLES:**

Jim Gerritsen
Wood Prairie Farm
www.woodprairie.com
49 Kinney Rd.
Bridgewater, ME 04735
order line: 800-829-9765
help line: 207-425-7741
info@woodprairie.com

**BOTANICAL ARK:**

Alan and Susan Carle
www.botanicalark.com
P.O. Box 354
Mossman, Queensland,
Australia 4873
tel: 61 (0)740 988 174
fax: 61 (0)740 988 173
info@botanicalark.com

**RECIPES**

**U.S. MAIL-ORDER SOURCES:**

Dean & DeLuca
www.deananddeluca.com
tel: 800-221-7714
fax: 800-721-4050
atyourservice@deandeluca.com

Formaggio Kitchen
www.formaggiokitchen.com
244 Huron Ave.
Cambridge, MA 02138
tel: 617-354-4750
info@formaggiokitchen.com

Williams-Sonoma
www.williams-sonoma.com
tel: 877-812-6235
fax: 702-353-2541

Zingerman's Deli
www.zingermans.com
422 Detroit St.
Ann Arbor, MI 48104
tel: 734-663-3354

**CHEFS**

Marino Family
Via Caduti per la Partria 25
12054 Cossano Belbo, Italy
tel: 39-0-141-88129
palmosei@libero.it
Garibaldi Family

Cà di Gòsita
Via Zerli 57
16040 Ne (GE), Italy
tel: 39 0185 339298

Elena Rovera
Cascina del Cornale
www.cornale.it
Corso Marconi
64-12050 Magliano Alfieri (CN),
Italy
tel: 39 0173 66669
cornale@cornale.it

Lothar Tubbesing
Restaurant Lachswehr
www.lachswehr.de
Lachswehrallee 38
23558 Lübeck, Germany
tel: 49 4510 84114
laxwehr@lynet.de

Georgette Dubos
Auberge de la Bidouze
Bidouze 32400 Riscle, France
tel: 33 0562 69 86 56

Tom and Giana Ferguson
Gubbeen House Farm
www.gubbeen.com
Schull, West Cork, Ireland
tel: +353 (0)28 28231
fax: +353 (0)28 28609
smokehouse@gubbeen.com
cheese@gubbeen.com

Steve Johnson
The Blue Room
One Kendall Square
Cambridge, MA 02139
tel: 617-494-9034

Ana Sortun
Oleana Restaurant
www.oleanarestaurant.com
134 Hampshire St.
Cambridge, MA 02139
tel: 617-661-0505

Daniel Boulud
Daniel
www.danielnyc.com
60 East 65th St.
New York, NY 10021
tel: 212-288-0033

Ben and Karen Barker
Magnolia Grill
1002 Ninth St.
Durham, NC 27705
tel: 919-286-3609

Rick Bayless
Topolobampo and Frontera Grill
445 N. Clark St.
Chicago, IL 60610
tel: 312-661-1434

Deborah Madison
964 Old Santa Fe Trail
Santa Fe, NM 87501
deborahmadison@earthlink.net

Alice Waters
Chez Panisse
www.chezpanisse.com
1517 Shattuck Ave.
Berkeley, CA 94709
tel: 510-548-5525

Judy Rodgers
Zuni Café
www.zunicafe.com
1658 Market St.
San Francisco, CA 94102
tel: 415-552-2522

Paul Bertolli
Oliveto Café and Restaurant
www.oliveto.com
5655 College Ave.
Oakland, CA 94618
tel: 510-547-5356

June Taylor
June Taylor Company
www.junetaylorjams.com
The Still-Room
2207 4th St.
Berkeley, CA 94710
tel: 510-923-1522
june@junetaylorjams.com

Elisabeth Prueitt
Tartine
www.tartinebakery.com
600 Guerrero St.
San Francisco, CA 94110
tel: 415-487-2600

**A**

Aioli, 117
Algarve, 46–48
Almonds
　Frangipane, 146
　Rochers, 170
American Cheese Society, 38–39
Anchovies, Zuni House-Cured, 149
Apples. *See also* Cider
　growing, 65–66, 69
　Pickled Herring with Apples and Crème
　　Fraîche, 95
Apricots
　Apricots in Almond Syrup, 161
　Apricot Tart, 145–46
　Fruit Focaccia, 169
Arcigola, 20, 22
The Ark, 22, 23–24, 26, 30. *See also*
　Botanical Ark
Aroostock County, 70, 72
Arugula Salad with Baked Ricotta and
　Cherry Tomatoes, 151
Auberge de la Bidouze, 63, 97, 100

**B**

Barboton d'Angeau with Creamed Spinach,
　119–20
Barker, Ben and Karen, 122–26
Barolo, 20
Basilicata, 31, 33–35
Battipaglia, 34
Bayless, Rick, 127–33
Beans
　Fava Bean Moussaka, 114
　Fideos with Special Chickpeas and
　　Saffron, 115
　Garbure, 99
　Hominy Succotash, 126
Bella, 34, 35
Berkeley, California, 138
Berries
　Blackberry Peach Summer Pudding, 152
　Röte Grütze, 96
Bertolli, Paul, 154–59, 165
Blackberry Peach Summer Pudding, 152
The Blue Room, 106, 107
Botanical Ark, 74–77
Botrytis, 56
Boulud, Daniel, 118–20
Bra, 16, 18, 19, 26
Bradstreet, Luke, 73
Brule, André, 97

**C**

Cabbage
　Garbure, 99
　Risotto Wrapped in Cabbage Leaves, 90
*Caciocavallo podolico*, 31–35
Cà di Gòsita, 16, 84
Cajeta (Goat's Milk Caramel), 133
Cambridge, Massachusetts, 106, 111
Caramel, Goat's Milk (Cajeta), 133
Carle, Alan and Susan, 74–77
Carpaccio of Veal with Old Balsamico, 155
Cascina del Cornale, 87, 92
Cheese
　artisan-made, 31–39

Arugula Salad with Baked Ricotta and
　Cherry Tomatoes, 151
　Baked Cheese with Winter Herbs, 102
　*caciocavallo podolico*, 31–35
　Gougères, 166
　Gubbeen, 101, 102
　*mozzarella di bufala*, 34
　raw milk in, 36
　Tortilla Soup with Pasilla Chilies, Fresh
　　Cheese, and Avocado, 128
　Vermont Shepherd, 36, 38–39
Chez Panisse, 26, 138, 139, 140, 142, 145,
　147, 154, 155
Chicago, 127
Chicken Cacciatore with Baked Potatoes,
　88–89
Chickpeas, Special, Fideos with Saffron and,
　115
Cider, 65–66, 69
Cod Braised with White Wine, Potatoes,
　and Escarole, 108
Conner, Adelé, 105
Corn
　Hominy Succotash, 126
　Posole with Chile Colorado, 135–36
　Soft-Shell Crab Bisque, 139
Cossano Belbo, 81
Crab
　blue, 51
　Soft-Shell Crab Bisque, 139
　stone, 51–54
Creamed Spinach (Crème d'Epinards), 120
Crepes, Buttered, with Caramel and Pecans,
　132–33
Cucumber and Purslane Salad with
　Sunflower Sprouts, 137

**D**

D'Amico, Maria Ines, 15–16, 84
Daniel, 118
Dietrich, Verna, 43–44
Di Gilio brothers, 31, 35
Dubos, Georgette, 97–100
Dubosc, André, 61–64, 97
Duck
　Garbure, 99
　Panfried Duck Breast with Sweet Sauce,
　　100
　Spelt Tagliatelle with Duck Giblets,
　　156–57
Durham, North Carolina, 122

**E**

Eggplant
　Fava Bean Moussaka, 114
Experimental Institute for Agricultural
　Research, 31, 33, 34–35

**F**

Farnum Hill, 69
Fava Bean Moussaka, 114
Ferguson, Tom and Giana, 101–5
Fiat, 17, 26
Fideos with Special Chickpeas and Saffron,
　115
Fish. *See individual varieties*
*Fleur de sel*, 46

Fo, Dario, 18
Focaccia, Fruit, 169
Frangipane, 146
Frontera Grill, 127
Fruit conserves and marmalades
　Apricots in Almond Syrup, 161
　Santa Rosa Plum Conserve, 163
　Thick-Cut Orange Marmalade, 164
Fruit Focaccia, 169

**G**

*Gambero Rosso*, 20
Garbure, 99
Garibaldi, Giuseppe, 15–16, 84–85
Gascony, 61, 64
Gerritsen, Jim, 70–73
Gers, 61, 62
Ghigo, Enzo, 26
Goat's Milk Caramel (Cajeta), 133
Gougères, 166
Grapes
　local French varieties of, 61–64
　Vidal, 55–56, 59
Gravlax with Citrus, 94
Gubbeen, 101, 102
Guerreiro, Maximino, 47

**H**

Ham
　artisan-made, 40, 44
　Roasted Fresh Ham with Salsa Verde,
　　124
　Tomato Soup with Poached Egg and
　　Serrano Ham, 123
Herring, Pickled, with Apples and Crème
　Fraîche, 95
Holmes, Chris, 72
Hominy Succotash, 126

**I**

Ice wine, 55–59
Inniskillin Winery, 56, 59

**J**

Joe's Stone Crab, 54
Johnson, Steve, 106–10

**K**

Kaiser, Karl, 55–59
Kramer, Torsten, 40–42, 43
Krumsville, Pennsylvania, 43
Kunast, Renate, 42

**L**

Lamb
　Barboton d'Angeau with Creamed
　　Spinach, 119–20
　Lamb Chops and Grilled Zucchini with
　　Vinegar and Mint, 150
　Lamb Steak with Turkish Spices and Fava
　　Bean Moussaka, 113
Langhe, 18, 19
La Torraca, Angela, 35
L'Etivas, 39
Liguria, 15, 84, 85
Longboat Key, Florida, 51, 54
Lübeck, 40–42, 93

**M**

Madernassa Pears with Birbet Wine, 92

Madison, Deborah, 134–37
Magnolia Grill, 122, 124
Major, Cindy and David, 36–39
Marino family, 81–82
Marmalades. *See* Fruit conserves and marmalades
Martins, Patrick, 26
McDonald's, 20, 22, 70
Meat, artisan-made, 40–44
Mesclun Greens with Sherry Vinaigrette, 110
Moliterno, 35
Monterey Bay Sardine Toasts with Garden Lettuces, 140
Moore's Stone Crab Restaurant, 53–54
Mornay Sauce, 114
Moussaka, Fava Bean, 114
*Mozzarella di bufala,* 34
Mulino Marino, 170
Mushroom Pasta Handkerchiefs, Wild, 142

**N**

Naples, 34
Navalho, João, 46–49
Necton, 46–49
New York City, 118
Niagara Peninsula, 55–56, 58

**O**

Oakland, California, 154, 160
Oleana Restaurant, 111
O'Leary, Michael, 51–54
Oliveto Café and Restaurant, 154
Orange Marmalade, Thick-Cut, 164
Osteria del Boccondivino, 19, 26

**P**

Paris, 22, 25
Pasta
    Fideos with Special Chickpeas and Saffron, 115
    Pasta Dough, 143
    Spelt Tagliatelle with Duck Giblets, 156–57
    Wild Mushroom Pasta Handkerchiefs, 142
Peach Summer Pudding, Blackberry, 152
Pears, Madernassa, with Birbet Wine, 92
Pecans, Buttered Crepes with Caramel and, 132–33
Pennsylvania Dutch country, 43–44
Pesto alla Genovese, 85
Petrini, Carlo, 18–20, 25, 26, 39, 134, 138
Piedmont, 18, 19, 26, 81, 87
Plaimont, 61–64
Plantains, Fried, with Chipotle Ketchup, 107
Plums
    Fruit Focaccia, 169
    Santa Rosa Plum Conserve, 163
Podolico cows, 31
Polenta with Bagna dl'Infern, 82
Pork Loin, Tomatillo-Braised, 130–31
Posole with Chile Colorado, 135–36
Potatoes
    Chicken Cacciatore with Baked Potatoes, 88–89
    Cod Braised with White Wine, Potatoes, and Escarole, 108
    Garbure, 99
    growing, 70, 72–73
    Yum, Yum, Pigs Bum, 104

Poverty Lane Orchards, 65
The Presidia, 22, 23–24, 30
Prueitt, Elisabeth, 165–70
Pudding, Blackberry Peach Summer, 152
Purslane and Cucumber Salad with Sunflower Sprouts, 137
Putney, Vermont, 36, 38

**Q**

Queensland, Australia, 74, 76

**R**

Rain forests, 74–77
Rance, Patrick, 38
Reif, Klaus, 58, 59
Restaurant Lachswehr, 41, 93, 94, 96
Ria Formosa, 47
Risotto Wrapped in Cabbage Leaves, 90
Robertson, Chad, 165
Robinson, Jancis, 64
Rochers, 170
Rodgers, Judy, 147–53
Rome, 20, 22, 33
Rose Geranium Custard Sauce, 153
Röte Grütze, 96
Rovera, Elena, 87–92
Rubino, Roberto, 33–35, 36, 39

**S**

Saint-Mont, 62, 97
Salads
    Arugula Salad with Baked Ricotta and Cherry Tomatoes, 151
    Cucumber and Purslane Salad with Sunflower Sprouts, 137
    Mesclun Greens with Sherry Vinaigrette, 110
    Monterey Bay Sardine Toasts with Garden Lettuces, 140
Salami, 40–41
Salmon
    Gravlax with Citrus, 94
Salone del Gusto, 17, 26
Salsa Verde, 124
Salt, 46–49
Sand Dabs, Tramezzino of, with Two Tomato Sauces, 159
San Francisco, 80, 147, 160, 165
Santa Fe, New Mexico, 134, 135
Santa Rosa Plum Conserve, 163
Sardine Toasts, Monterey Bay, with Garden Lettuces, 140
Sardo, Piero, 33
Sausage
    artisan-made, 40–44
    salami, 40–41
    Yum, Yum, Pigs Bum, 104
Schull, 101
Scones, Wholemeal West Cork, from Adelé's Café, 105
Scott, Alan, 165
Shellfish, 51–54
Slow Food
    convivia (chapters) of, 16–17, 23, 25
    founding of, 18–19, 22
    goals of, 16–18
    initiatives of, 22–25, 30
    international following, 25–26
    Salone del Gusto (food fair), 17, 26
    symbol of, 22
    Web site, 23
Slow Food Award, 22, 25, 30, 47

Soft-Shell Crab Bisque, 139
Sortun, Ana, 111–17
Soups
    Garbure, 99
    Soft-Shell Crab Bisque, 139
    Tomato Soup with Poached Egg and Serrano Ham, 123
    Tortilla Soup with Pasilla Chilies, Fresh Cheese, and Avocado, 128
    Yum, Yum, Pigs Bum, 104
Spelt Tagliatelle with Duck Giblets, 156–57
Spinach, Creamed (Crème d'Epinards), 120
Stone crabs, 51–54
Succotash, Hominy, 126

**T**

Tangren, Alan, 145
Tart, Apricot, 145–46
Tartine, 165
Taylor, June, 160–64, 165
*Testaroli,* 15, 84
Tomatillo-Braised Pork Loin, 130–31
Tomatoes
    Arugula Salad with Baked Ricotta and Cherry Tomatoes, 151
    Tomato Soup with Poached Egg and Serrano Ham, 123
    Tramezzino of Sand Dabs with Two Tomato Sauces, 159
Topolobampo, 127
Tortilla Soup with Pasilla Chilies, Fresh Cheese, and Avocado, 128
TradiSal, 49
Tramezzino of Sand Dabs with Two Tomato Sauces, 159
Tubbesing, Lothar and Heike, 41, 42, 93–96
Turin, 17

**V**

Veal
    Carpaccio of Veal with Old Balsamico, 155
    Risotto Wrapped in Cabbage Leaves, 90
Verdelho, Vitor, 47
Vermont Shepherd, 36, 38–39
Vidal grapes, 55–56, 59
*Vin de pays,* 62

**W**

Waters, Alice, 26, 134, 138–46, 154, 165
Wine
    artisan-made, 55–64
    ice, 55–59
    Madernassa Pears with Birbet Wine, 92
    ratings of, 20
    *vin de pays,* 62
Wood, Stephen, 65–69
Wood Prairie Farm, 72, 73

**Y**

Yum, Yum, Pigs Bum, 104

**Z**

Ziraldo, Donald, 56
Zucchini, Grilled, and Lamb Chops with Vinegar and Mint, 150
Zuni Café, 147, 149
Zuni House-Cured Anchovies, 149

# TABLE OF EQUIVALENTS

*The exact equivalents in the following tables have been rounded for convenience.*

## LIQUID/DRY MEASURES

| U.S. | METRIC |
| --- | --- |
| ¼ teaspoon | 1.25 milliliters |
| ½ teaspoon | 2.5 milliliters |
| 1 teaspoon | 5 milliliters |
| 1 tablespoon (3 teaspoons) | 15 milliliters |
| 1 fluid ounce (2 tablespoons) | 30 milliliters |
| ¼ cup | 60 milliliters |
| ⅓ cup | 80 milliliters |
| ½ cup | 120 milliliters |
| 1 cup | 240 milliliters |
| 1 pint (2 cups) | 480 milliliters |
| 1 quart (4 cups, 32 ounces) | 960 milliliters |
| 1 gallon (4 quarts) | 3.84 liters |
| | |
| 1 ounce (by weight) | 28 grams |
| 1 pound | 454 grams |
| 2.2 pounds | 1 kilogram |

## LENGTH

| U.S. | METRIC |
| --- | --- |
| ⅛ inch | 3 millimeters |
| ¼ inch | 6 millimeters |
| ½ inch | 12 millimeters |
| 1 inch | 2.5 centimeters |

## OVEN TEMPERATURE

| FAHRENHEIT | CELSIUS | GAS |
| --- | --- | --- |
| 250 | 120 | ½ |
| 275 | 140 | 1 |
| 300 | 150 | 2 |
| 325 | 160 | 3 |
| 350 | 180 | 4 |
| 375 | 190 | 5 |
| 400 | 200 | 6 |
| 425 | 220 | 7 |
| 450 | 230 | 8 |
| 475 | 240 | 9 |
| 500 | 260 | 10 |